Contents

yasmin Erdogan
10 a

Unit 1 Love life!

1 Who's who? ▸ pp. 6–7

Complete the sentences with names of the characters.

1 Toby and ______ are brother and sister.

2 ______ and ______ are old friends.

3 ______ and ______ are best friends.

4 ______ has a girlfriend.

5 ______ would like to go out with ______ – but he doesn't know.

6 Everybody likes ______ because he's cool.

2 Welcome to West Street ▸ pp. 6–7

a) *Read pp. 6–7 of your student's book again. Are the statements below true or false? Tick a letter.*

		True	False
1	Bex would like to go out with Ed.	T ✓	Y
2	Peanut hasn't got a girlfriend.	P	K
3	Minty always tries hard to look good.	A	T
4	Peanut and Ed have known each other a long time.	I	M
5	Bex doesn't care much about her appearance.	I	L
6	Minty is a confident and positive person.	N	T
7	Bex is Toby's girlfriend.	N	U
8	Minty has a good sense of humour and is relaxed.	T	P
9	Peanut is interested in all kinds of things and knows a lot.	H	U
10	People like Peanut although he isn't as out-going as the others.	I	P

b) *If your answers are correct, in the right order the letters give you the name of a West Street character:*

____

c) *How might the West Street story go on? Write a few sentences.*

____

____

____

3 Choose a friend ▸ pp. 6–7

Which boy and which girl of the West Street five might you choose to be in your circle of friends? Think about their characters and interests, maybe about their appearance. Say what you think is positive about them and why. Write a paragraph in your exercise book.

I think I would choose … and … to be in my circle of friends. First, …

4 Leo's problem ▸ p. 9 • WB (pp. 75–76)

Read about Leo's problem. Then think about the situation from the point of view of both Leo's former and his present girlfriend. What advice would you give Leo? Write your ideas in your exercise book (about 100 words). For help you can read pp. 8–9 in your student's book again.

Hi,
My name's Leo and I have this problem:
I was with Katie, a girl from my school, for nine months. It was a really good relationship. Then her family moved to South America because of her dad's job. At first we kept in touch by phone and computer, but I guess I didn't want to be alone, and Katie had no idea when they would be coming back to the UK. After a time I started going out with another girl, Ella, also from our school, and contact with Katie became less and less.
Now, after a year and a half in Brazil, Katie and her family have returned unexpectedly, and she is back at our school – in the same class as Ella.
I don't know what to do. I find myself thinking about Katie more and more, and when I see her I just feel the same as I always used to when we were together. I'm still with Ella, so I know this isn't fair. But what can I do? I can't help my feelings for Katie. I guess our relationship was never really over. It was just the miles between us.
I don't know how she feels. We haven't really spoken to each other. It's difficult. I expect she knows about Ella, as they are both in the same class. I hate this situation. I really need to know if Katie has another boyfriend or if she still likes me. Do we have a second chance?
What should I do?

B, pp. –61

5 WORDS Describing someone's character ▸ p. 10

a) *The words in the box describe a person's character. Make two lists: positive and negative. Then add at least three more words to each list.*

ambitious • arrogant • boring • charming • cheeky • confident • easy-going • funny • greedy • intolerant • lazy • loyal • lovable • punctual • relaxed • reliable • rude • useless • violent

☺ ambitious, ______

☹ arrogant, ______

b) *Complete the sentences about yourself. Use words from a) above.*

I always try to be ______

I know that I am sometimes ______

I hope I am never ______

0305

Now you

Which positive qualities are the most important for you in a best friend? Which negative qualities are in your opinion the worst? Why? Use the words in exercise 5 and your own words. Write a few sentences.

For me it's important that a friend is ______________________

____

____

6 Band night (Present tenses) ▸ p. 10 • WB (p. 77)

Tim is describing a photo which he's sending to an e-friend. Here is part of his e-mail. Complete the text with the correct forms of the verbs in brackets. Use the ***simple present*** *or the* ***present progressive****.*

1 I *'m sending* (send) you a photo of me with my band. We *call* (call) ourselves *Westbound* – I ______ (not remember) how we chose that name. We just ______ (think) it ______ (sound) good.

2 Here we ______ (rehearse) at the youth club. There's a local band competition in two weeks. We ______ (enter) it, of course. Maybe we'll win.

3 We're pretty good. We usually ______ (practise) twice a week and we ______ (write) our own songs, of course. At the moment we ______ (write) our first album. We ______ (work) really hard on it.

4 So who's who? Well, the guy on drums is Brad. He ______ (know) a lot about sound, recording so he ______ (record) our album when it's finished.

5 The boy who ______ (wear) the orange shirt is Dave. And I'm the guy with the electric guitar.

6 The girl on the right is Fran, my girlfriend. She ______ (sing) and ______ (play) the guitar. In the photo she ______ (sing) our new song. She ______ (want) to train as a nurse – that is, if we ______ (not become) rich and famous with our band – joke!

0406

7 EVERYDAY ENGLISH SPEAKING
Keeping a conversation going

▸ p. 11 • WB (pp. 74–75)

a) What is important if you want to keep a conversation going? Tick four more boxes.

1	Find out the person's name, where he/she lives, etc.	✔	*5*	Give the person lots of compliments[1] about their looks or their clothes.	☐
2	Make comments that show you are interested or surprised.	☐	*6*	Find out about the person's likes and interests.	☐
3	Ask personal questions.	☐	*7*	Talk about yourself a lot.	☐
4	Ask open questions with when, where, what, etc.	☐	*8*	Change the subject if the conversation is not going well.	☐

b) Noah would like to get to know Amy. How could he keep Amy interested in the conversation? Circle A or B.

Noah Hi, I'm Noah.
Amy Hi.
Noah (A): Sorry, what was your name?
B: Er ..., and who are you?
Amy I'm Amy.
Noah A: Oh. OK. Well, I'm 16 and I live in ...
B: Oh, that's a nice name. My sister's called Amy. Do you live around here?
Amy Yes, but actually we're new in town.
Noah A: I thought I hadn't seen you here before. Where are you from?
B: Oh, er ... I see.
Amy We moved here from Liverpool just three weeks ago.
Noah A: I don't think I've been there. Maybe when I was a kid.
B: Liverpool. Right! Now that is a great place – for music too.
Amy That's true. We have some great clubs.
Noah A: What kind of music are you into?
B: Good.
Amy R&B mainly. Some dance-pop too.
Noah A : Oh, so you like Rihanna and Beyoncé. Cool. Me too. And what about films?
B: Oh, my last girlfriend liked R&B too.
Amy Oh, I love the cinema. But I don't watch every new film.
Noah A: Most films are stupid. I mean, ... well, ...
B: No, neither[2] do I. I don't have the time or the money for that. But have you seen ...?

c) Write six open questions which you could use to keep a conversation going. Ideas: music, films, TV, sport, travel, school, free time, after-school jobs, future plans.

What kind of music do you like?
____
____
____

d) Write an interesting conversation between Jack and Sienna, two UK teenagers. Use the conversation skills that you have practised in a)–c): Write down some useful phrases, prepare some topics to talk about, think of useful questions. Write in your exercise book. Prepare to act out your dialogue in class with a partner.

WB, pp. 3–55

[1]compliment ['kɒmplɪmənt] *Kompliment* [2]neither ['naɪðə] *auch nicht*

8 Film reviews ▸ pp. 12–13

a) Look at the film reviews on pp. 12–13 of your student's book again. Which statements match the four films? Write the numbers 2–14 under the film titles.

500 Days of Summer	Bend it like Beckham	Twilight	Juno
	1,		

1 This very funny film is set in the UK.
2 The teenage girl in this film has just moved to a new school.
3 A pregnant teenager plays the main role in this film.
4 The film is based on a best-selling novel.
5 The soundtrack is a perfect mix of Indian and British music.
6 This film is set in L.A.
7 The teenage girl in this film has a dad who supports her.
8 This film is a fantasy drama.
9 The film shows the problems of living in two very different cultures.
10 The special effects in this film are excellent.
11 You could call this film an anti-romance.
12 Getting pregnant is not the greatest danger in this relationship.
13 Marc Webber directed this film.
14 Difficult teenager-parent relationships are also a topic in this film.

b) You want to tell an e-friend that you have seen a review of the film Juno. Write an e-mail telling your friend what you know about the film. Use present tenses for the story. Say why you think you would like to see the film. Remember your writing skills for informal letters. Write about 100 words in your exercise book.

9 LISTENING A radio phone-in ▸ p. 14 • WB (p. 72) 2

Test

Four young people talk about their problems on a radio phone-in. Before you listen, read the advice (statements 1–6 below) carefully. Then listen to the problems and choose the advice which fits each problem best. Write a number after each name. Two pieces of advice do not fit any of the problems.

Beth: ☐ Matthew: ☐ Simon: ☐ Lauren: ☐

1 You don't seem to be happy. This girl is slowly killing your relationship, so end it yourself.
2 It may be just a flirt, it may be more. But if he has a girlfriend, don't encourage him. Keep away.
3 Don't break up a friendship for a relationship that probably won't last anyway. Both of you should dump this guy.
4 You want this boy as a boyfriend, not just a mate. But you can't make this happen. For the moment just enjoy his friendship and give it time.
5 Maybe he likes you too, but he's too shy to talk to you when you're in a group. Try to catch him alone and start a conversation. Then just see how it goes.
6 Maybe you should tell your girlfriend about your problem. You won't lose her if your relationship is as good as you say. Secret[1] feelings are often not as strong when you talk about them, and maybe the new girl has a boyfriend anyway.

WB, pp. 48–52

0608

[1]secret ['si:krət] *geheim*

10 READING Dive[1] ▸ p. 14 • WB (pp. 72–73)

a) Look at the pictures. What do you think the text may be about? Write a few sentences in your exercise book.

The pictures show ... *Maybe the girl ...* *It looks as if ...*

b) Look at the text quickly. What kind of text is it? Tick a box.

A book review ☐ An online blog ☐ A TV film review ☐

Dive ★★★★★

The TV drama *Dive* (2010) is set in a small seaside town in England. The film was written and directed by TV author Dominic Savage. It tells the story of Lindsey (young star Aisling Loftus), a schoolgirl athlete, who is training hard to be chosen for the British diving team at the London 2012 Olympics.

Lindsey's father, who supports his daughter with her strict training programme, leaves home suddenly and her mother's new boyfriend moves in. Lindsey is upset, and out of protest she misses her diving training to hang out in the park with a group of beer-drinking classmates, something she has never done before. But this one time changes Lindsey's life and her dream – she gets pregnant. The father is Robert (fine young actor Jack O'Connell), an arrogant but popular 16-year-old, who Lindsey doesn't know well.

The film shows how Lindsey and her boyfriend try to manage[2] the new situation and their lives. Robert's father is angry. Lindsey decides to give up her Olympic dream and have the baby. The teenagers argue and break up, but they come together again before the birth. In spite of[3] the difficulties of living together, the young parents grow in their new roles. Lindsey's sporting ambition[4] is still alive, and she begins her diving training again, watched by Robert and the baby.

This is not a typical story of broken homes and lost dreams. It is realistic and unsentimental, but optimistic. It is brilliantly acted and beautifully filmed. On the negative side, the violin soundtrack is sometimes over-used.

Although *Dive* is about a teenage pregnancy, it is a story for everybody. Highly recommended.

c) Now read the text carefully and tick the correct statements.

In this review the reader is informed about ...

1 what kind of film it is. ☑
2 who wrote and directed the film. ☐
3 where the film is set. ☐
4 the year the film was made. ☐
5 what the film is about. ☐
6 who the main actors are. ☐
7 the supporting actors[5] and their roles. ☐
8 the quality of the acting. ☐
9 which qualities make the film special. ☐
10 how much the film cost to make. ☐
11 the soundtrack. ☐
12 special effects. ☐
13 who will like the film. ☐
14 what other films the main actors have made. ☐

WB, pp. 62–65
0710

[1]dive [daɪv] *(Kopf-)Sprung, Tauchen* [2]manage ['mænɪdʒ] *bewältigen* [3]in spite of [spaɪt] *trotz* [4]ambition [æm'bɪʃn] *Ehrgeiz* [5]supporting actor [sə'pɔːtɪŋ] *Nebendarsteller/in*

11 WORDS Film words ▸ p. 14

a) *Write the film words in two lists: kind of film and words to describe a film.*

action • adventure • amazing • awful • boring • clever • comedy • crime drama • funny • historical drama • horror film • musical • police drama • realistic • romantic • sad • scary • science fiction • stupid • terrible • thriller • war • violent • western

Different kinds of films:

action, ______

______

We can describe films as:

amazing, ______

______

b) *What kind of films do you like best, and why? What kind of films do you not like, and why? Write four sentences. Use words from both lists in a).*

I really like/I never watch … because they're usually … and …

1 ______

2 ______

3 ______

0811 4 ______

12 WRITING A film I really enjoyed ▸ p. 14 • WB (pp. 75–76)

Think of a film that you really enjoyed. Write a review about it. You can use the internet for names (director, actors, characters' names). Look at exercises 8 and 10 (WB, pp. 6–7) and the reviews in your student's book (pp. 12–13) for ideas. In your review, mention the following:

- the film's title
- when and where the film was made
- the kind of film it is (comedy, musical, etc.)
- the setting (place or country, time: past, present, future)
- names of the main actors
- the storyline, plot (main events)
- the main characters (appearance, personal qualities, age)
- topic, theme
- soundtrack or special effects
- who will like the film (teenagers, adults, kids)
- your personal opinion: what makes the film special, what you liked best, why you would recommend it

INFO BOX

Here are some of the most successful US film productions worldwide:

2010 *Alice in Wonderland*
2009 *Avatar*
2008 *The Dark Knight*
2007 *Pirates of the Caribbean: At World's End*

Avatar (directed by James Cameron) made more than $2.5 billion[1], followed by *Titanic* (James Cameron, 1997) with more than $1.8 billion.

Use present tenses. Write in your exercise book. The phrases below will help you.

A film that I really enjoyed is (title).
It is a (kind of film) and it was directed by …
It stars …
The film tells the story of …
At the beginning/Later/At the end …
My favourite scene/part is when/where …
My favourite character is … because …
There is a happy ending when/because …
The acting/soundtrack/photography/dialogue is brilliant …
The plot is fast-moving, exciting, realistic …
To sum up, I love this film because …
I would give it … stars out of five …

WB, pp. 56–61

[1] billion [ˈbɪljən] *Milliarde*

13 SPEAKING Friends

▸ p. 14 • WB (pp. 74–75)

a) Choose one of the pictures. Describe it and say what you think the situation is. How do you think the girl in the foreground is feeling? Make notes in your exercise book and speak for about two minutes.

1

2

b) Prepare spoken answers to these questions and give a three-minute talk.

WB, pp. 53–55

1 What do you do with your friends in your free time?
2 Why do you like your friends?
3 Are your friends important to you? Do you help each other? How?
4 Do you think it's better to have lots of friends or just one or two really good friends?

14 REVISION Tim and Nina (Past tenses)

▸ p. 15 • WB (p. 78)

*Complete what Nina says about her boyfriend Tim. Put the verbs in the **simple past** or **past progressive**.*

Tim is a really great boyfriend. He's so relaxed and he has a great sense of humour, but of course nobody is perfect and Tim isn't always reliable. Last Friday we __wanted__ (want) to see the new action film starring Matt Damon.

The film ________ (start) at 7.30, so at 7.20 I ________ (wait) for him outside the cinema. Lots of people ________ (stand) in the ticket queue.

It ________ (rain) too. I ________ (try) to call Tim on his mobile, but he ________ (not answer). I ________ (think) perhaps he ________ (come) by car and was stuck in a traffic jam. Then, a few minutes later, he ________ (call) me.

He ________ (say) he ________ (stand) outside the *Odeon* – with cold feet.

He ________ (wait) for me. But the film ________ (show) at the *Apollo*!

Typical Tim!

0914

15 WRITING A first date

▸ p. 15 • WB (pp. 75–76)

Test

a) Tell the story in the pictures. Choose names for the characters. Make notes on the situation in each picture. You can use the phrases below or your own ideas. Use the **simple past** *and the* **past progressive** *for the main tenses. Write about 100 words in your exercise book.*

1	2	3
first date – stand in front of the cinema – wait – look at watch – call on mobile	see someone else waiting – have same problem – angry – start a conversation	talk about films and music – great first date

b) Write the dialogue between the two young people for the three scenes. Remember to use your speaking skills 'How to keep a conversation going'. Here are some ideas for scene 1:

WB, pp. 56–61

Girl: (on phone) Hello. This is … I'm waiting in front of the cinema. Are you on the way? Or is there a problem? Call me back, please.

Boy: Excuse me. My name's … I just heard your call. You're waiting for someone who hasn't come. I'm …

16 MEDIATION 17 Again

▸ p. 15 • WB (p. 77)

Test

Read the summary of the 2009 teen comedy '17 Again'. Explain to a German friend, whose English isn't as good as yours, what the film is about.

In this teen comedy Mike O'Donnell (Zac Efron) is 17 and is the star of his high school basketball team. He has a promising future to look forward to, as he has hopes of getting a college scholarship[1]. Then he discovers that his girlfriend Scarlet is pregnant. He decides to give up his college future and marry her. Twenty years later his wife wants to divorce him, his two kids hate him and he is unsuccessful in his job. He ends up living with his former best school friend Ned. Dissatisfied[2] with his life, Mike starts thinking 'What if …?' and wishes he could relive his life. Mysteriously, he gets the chance to be 17 again, and suddenly he finds himself in high school – with his kids.

WB, pp. 66–67

1016

[1]scholarship ['skɒləʃɪp] *Stipendium* [2]dissatisfied [dɪs'sætɪsfaɪd] *unzufrieden*

17 Extra WORKING WITH THE TEXT The Absolutely True Diary ... ▸ pp. 16–19

a) Read 'Pancakes of doom' again (student's book, pp. 17–19). Then put the events in the correct order. Write numbers 2–10 in the boxes.

1 At the pancake diner Arnold orders lots of food and drinks. ☐
2 Penelope doesn't want Arnold to hitchhike home. ☐
3 Arnold goes to the bathroom because he feels sick. ☐
4 Later, Penelope asks Arnold if he is poor. ☐
5 Roger asks Penelope and Arnold to go to a pancake diner with him and some friends. *1*
6 Arnold tells Roger that he has forgotten his wallet. ☐
7 Penelope wants to go, but Arnold is scared because he has only got five dollars. ☐
8 Penelope tells Roger the truth about Arnold. ☐
9 Roger gives Arnold forty dollars. ☐
10 Roger drives Arnold home. ☐

b) Answer the questions on the text.

1 L. 3 (p. 16) of the text says that Arnold makes a 'brave decision'. What is his decision and why is it brave?

2 Arnold is surprised that he is popular with the kids at his new school. Explain this in a few sentences.

3 Describe the 'big dreams' that Arnold and Penelope have.

c) Extra Famous people often come from poor or difficult family backgrounds, but they succeed because of their ambition[1], talent and hard work. Examples are US President Barack Obama or singer/actress Jennifer Lopez. Think of more examples of famous people, past or present, who also had difficult childhoods but succeeded. Write a few sentences.

1118
1119

[1]ambition [æm'bɪʃn] *Ehrgeiz*

Exam Check

1 LISTENING Friends on the net 3

You are going to hear five teenagers talking about making friends on the internet. You will hear the recording once. First read the statements below. Listen and choose the correct statement for each person. Write the correct letters in the boxes. There is one statement more than you need.

Richard: ☐ Angie: ☐ Robin: ☐ Lisa: ☐ Josie: ☐

A You can practise languages and learn about other cultures on the internet.

B There's nothing better than the internet for making lots of new friends.

C When you sit at the computer alone, you don't make real friends because you can't speak to people.

D You can find old friends again on social networking sites.

E You can lose friends if you spend too much time on the net.

F You can join groups of people with exactly the same interests as you.

2 LISTENING Voicemail messages 4

a) Robert has four voicemail messages. First read the statements below. Then listen to the messages and tick the correct box.

	True	False	Not given
Message 1			
1 If Rob joins his friends, there will be five of them.	☐	☐	☐
2 The film starts at seven thirty.	☐	☐	☐
3 The *Odeon* cinema is in Winslow Street.	☐	☐	☐
Message 2			
4 Becca has lost her mobile.	☐	☐	☐
5 Sandy and Becca wanted to go to a concert on the Tube.	☐	☐	☐
6 Becca can call Sandy on 02072877355.	☐	☐	☐
Message 3			
7 Jay and Rob play in a band.	☐	☐	☐
8 Jay suggests changing the next band meeting to Wednesday.	☐	☐	☐
9 It's Adam's birthday on Tuesday.	☐	☐	☐
Message 4			
10 Mel wants Rob to help her with her computer.	☐	☐	☐
11 She'll pay him for his help.	☐	☐	☐
12 Mel's number is 07760049872.	☐	☐	☐

b) Listen to the recording again and check your answers.

3 LISTENING Talking about free time 5

a) *You are going to hear a conversation about free time. First read the statements about Trish, Fran, Scott and Todd (1–12). Then listen to the recording and complete the sentences.*

1 Trish likes Kylie Minogue and ______________________ music.

2 Trish likes to watch *Neighbours*, which is on TV at ______________________ on weekdays.

3 *Neighbours* has been on TV for about ______________________ years.

4 Fran's ______________________ watches *Neighbours* too.

5 The soap *Home and Away* is on network ______________________ at __________ every day.

6 Fran's ______________________ watches *Home and Away*.

7 Scott watches tennis and ______________________ on TV.

8 Todd likes to watch ______________________ on TV.

9 Todd is into ______________________ sports.

10 He goes ______________________ twice a week.

11 Todd asks Scott to join him at the club on ______________________ after __________ .

12 Scott says he could get the ______________________ bus.

b) *Listen again and check your answers.*

4 SPEAKING Dumped

Describe the picture. Make notes and talk for about three minutes. You can record what you say.

1 How do you think the girl is feeling?

____

____

2 What has happened?

____

____

3 Do you think it's OK to end a friendship or a relationship by text message?

____

____

4 What advice would you give the girl to make her feel better?

____

____

5 SPEAKING A cartoon

Talk about the cartoon. The questions in the box below will help you.

"YOUR MOTHER AND I FOUND OUT YOU'VE BEEN BLOGGING. WE DON'T KNOW WHAT THAT MEANS, BUT WE'D LIKE YOU TO STOP."

What can you see? • What is happening? • What does the father think of his son? • What does the son think of his father? • What is the cartoon's message? • Do you agree with what the cartoon artist wants to say?

6 SPEAKING Comparing photos

Choose a photo and talk about it. Then compare it with the other photo in a few sentences. Discuss advantages and disadvantages of going on holiday with friends and going on holiday with your family. Which do you think is better and why? Also think of four questions to ask a partner about this topic. Make notes in your exercise book and talk for about three minutes.

1

2

7 WRITING A questionnaire

Answer the questions. Write about 100 words.

QUESTIONNAIRE: FRIENDSHIP

1 How important is friendship to you? ______

2 What do you think is better and why: lots of friends or only a few really good friends? ______

3 How often do you see your best friend? ______

4 How much time do you spend with your friends every week? ______

5 How long have you known your best friend? ______

6 Which qualities do you look for in a friend? Explain why. ______

7 What hobbies or interests do you share with your friends? ______

8 Nobody is perfect. What might cause you to break off a friendship? Give an example. ______

8 WRITING A picture story

Tell the story in the pictures. Write two or three sentences for each picture. You can use the words given.

1

Sophie – boyfriend – dump – sad and angry – new girlfriend?

2

phone best friend – cry – advice – don't sit at home – go somewhere

3

decide – visit cousin – weekend – go on moped

4

leave home – on moped – rain

5

an hour later – stop – café – nice young guy

6

sit – next table – chat – laugh

7

leave café together – will meet again the next day – forget old boyfriend

9 WRITING What's your opinion?

Choose one of the following statements and write your opinion about it. Give reasons and examples where possible and sum up your opinion. Write about 120 words.

1 You can learn a lot about friends and relationships from soap operas.
2 Being a teenager has its good and bad points.
3 Teenagers spend too much time on computer and video games.

10 WRITING A report

Choose one of the following topics and write a report of about 120 words.

1 Our last family holiday
2 My favourite film
3 A good day in town with my friends

11 MEDIATION A letter to a problem page

a) You read about a problem in a UK teen magazine. You also read the advice.

I can't forget him

I went out with a really nice boy for four months. We shared the same interests and had a lot of fun together. Just when I thought I had found the boy of my dreams, he suddenly said he just wanted to be friends. He dumped me without giving me a reason. That was four weeks ago. He doesn't answer my calls or e-mails. I expect he's dating someone new and doesn't want to tell me. I'm really unhappy because I miss him and I can't forget him. What should I do?

Charlotte, 16

Dear Charlotte,

There's only one good way to forget an unhappy relationship – find a new exciting one! But first, get busy doing things that help to get HIM out of your life. Throw away or delete photos, videos, phone numbers and e-mail addresses, letters and e-mails, favourite song, anything that reminds you of the time you were together. Don't play romantic music or watch romantic films. Don't listen to song texts about unhappy love – and don't watch happy couples on the street! When you find yourself thinking about him, call a friend, help in the kitchen, read a newspaper or do homework – anything to make you think of other things. Don't go to bed until you are really tired. Otherwise you may lie awake for hours – and he isn't worth[1] it.

Now that you have more time alone, do the things you never had time for when you were together. Get out there! Do sports, join a club, go to the cinema with your girl friends. Don't go to places you used to go to with HIM. Go to new places and meet new people!

Remember, this happens to everyone at some time, so talk to your friends and let them help you too.

Your mag team

b) You have a German friend who is in the same situation as Charlotte. In a short e-mail to your friend, write German notes about the advice in the magazine.

12 MEDIATION Adverts

You are looking for an apprenticeship. Your cousin in the UK is also looking for an apprenticeship. You often exchange notes about what interests you. Write notes in English about the adverts below.

1 Für Neueröffnung unseres Friseursalons im Zentrum Hamburgs suchen wir ab sofort eine/n **Auszubildende/n (m/w)** für unser junges Team. Kontaktaufnahme bitte unter 0173/624 8942 od. schriftlich an B. Thiele, Alster Haarmoden, Wagnerstr. 1

2 Gehobenes 4-Sterne Hotel in Hamburg sucht ab sof. auszubildende/n **Köchin/Koch** für unsere moderne Großküche. Erfahrung von Vorteil. Bewerbung telefonisch unter 040/401 6927

3 Möchten Sie eine gesicherte Zukunft als **KFZ-Mechaniker/in?** Für unseren großen Reparaturbetrieb suchen wir ab sofort Auszubildende. Wir erwarten einen guten Schulabschluss (Mittlere Reife), gutes technisches Verständnis und Interesse an Kundenbetreuung. Ein absolviertes Praktikum in einer Kfz-Werkstatt wäre von Vorteil. Bewerbung bitte schriftlich an S. Mack, Lindenstraße 2, 20144 Hamburg

4 Für unsere Filiale in Hamburg suchen wir zum 01.08.2012 auszubildende **Bankangestellte**. Sie haben gute Noten in Mathematik, Deutsch und Englisch (Mittlere Reife), sind teamfähig, zuverlässig, haben ein sicheres Auftreten und Interesse am Kunden-Service. Wir bieten eine praxisorienterte Ausbildung in einem modernen Arbeitsumfeld.Bewerbung bitte an BSK Bank Hamburg, Lenzstr. 9

[1]worth [wɜːθ] *wert*

READING

13 READING Daniel's blog

a) First read the whole text. Then complete the tasks.

Hi, friends!

Well, here I am in Oxford! My old friend Max and I are at a tennis camp – and it's brilliant! Two weeks of tennis, English language and culture, sightseeing and entertainment! My English is better already – as proof I'm writing my blog in English! Here's what's been happening in the past few days.

Sunday, 1st August
We arrived at Heathrow from Cologne, were picked up and taken to Oxford in a minibus – with four annoying 10-year-olds (on the kids' course). After a good hour of driving, we arrived in Oxford – couldn't wait to get rid of the screaming kids! Our accommodation[1] is great, nice student rooms in the Queen's College. We could have stayed with a host family or at a B&B, but we thought college would be more fun. It is fun – but we have to be in bed at 10.30 – very uncool! In the evening there was a barbecue, so we met the other students. Some are from the UK, but mainly from other EU countries and Japan. International atmosphere. Cool! Max has fallen in love with a Spanish girl called Maria!

Monday, 2nd August
Had a great English breakfast (sausages, beans, eggs, bacon). First, the coaches watched us play and they put us into groups. Maria was put in the same group as me – sorry, Max, not my fault. There's also Sven from Sweden, Jean-Paul from somewhere near Paris, Anna from Poland, and a Greek girl called Elena. We have to speak English together. In my group we're all 16 to 18. English conversation in the afternoon with our teacher, Nina, was cool too. Really relaxed. Just eight in our group, laughed a lot. Max didn't say much – couldn't take his eyes off Maria, but she doesn't seem to be interested.

Tuesday, 3rd August
Today I was bored with the discussion on tactics, strategy and mental attitude – I just want to play for fun, nothing too serious. But after lunch we did a city tour by open-top bus. Great! We saw all the city highlights, like some of the world's oldest colleges, including Merton and Magdalen (pronounced 'Maudlin'). Christ Church, founded in 1500 and something, is very special. Really beautiful! I think the guide said that 13 British prime ministers had studied there. And parts of the Harry Potter books were filmed there, in the Great Hall. After the tour we went into town with the guys in my group and Anna. We looked in the music stores. Then we saw Maria and Elena in a shoe shop, so suddenly Max thought he needed new trainers ...! In the evening we all watched a DVD and chatted.

Thursday, 5th August
More sausages for breakfast, more tennis with Maria, more English conversation. In the evening we played volleyball or football. Some of us seem to be better at football than at tennis – including me!

Saturday, 7th August
In the morning we had a boring video analysis of each player in our tennis groups – not cool when you try to do a perfect stroke but miss the ball! Nobody is perfect, so we laughed a lot. Tomorrow we're all going on a trip to London. Brilliant! I'll tell you about it in my next blog.

Daniel

b) Choose A, B or C.

1 The blog is ...

- A from an English boy doing a tennis course in Oxford.
- B from a German boy doing an English course in Oxford.
- C from a German boy doing a tennis course with English classes in Oxford.

2 The journey from Heathrow to Oxford took ...

- A an hour.
- B less than an hour.
- C more than an hour.

[1]accommodation [əˌkɒmə'deɪʃn] *Unterkunft*

3 Daniel and Max are staying ...

A at a bed and breakfast place.

B in college rooms.

C with an Oxford family.

4 Daniel is ...

A 16 years old.

B between 16 and 18.

C over 18.

5 In Daniel's tennis group there are ... students altogether.

A five

B six

C eight

Christ Church, Oxford

c) Tick the correct box.

	True	False	Not given
1 Daniel has known Max a long time.	☐	☐	☐
2 Max plays tennis very well.	☐	☐	☐
3 Elena is from Athens.	☐	☐	☐
4 The name of the English teacher is Anna.	☐	☐	☐
5 Daniel doesn't take the tennis course too seriously.	☐	☐	☐
6 Merton and Magdalen are former British prime ministers.	☐	☐	☐
7 Scenes from the Harry Potter films were filmed at Christ Church.	☐	☐	☐
8 Max wanted to buy new trainers because Maria was in the shoe shop.	☐	☐	☐
9 One evening Daniel and Max went to the cinema.	☐	☐	☐
10 Tennis is the game that Daniel plays best.	☐	☐	☐

d) Answer the questions.

1 What nationality are the following people?

Maria: ____________ Nina: ____________ Max: ____________ Anna: ____________

Sven: ____________ Jean-Paul: ____________ Elena: ____________

2 What did Daniel really like about his stay in Oxford? Write five things.

____

____

____

3 What didn't Daniel like very much? Write three things.

____

____

____

____

14 USE OF LANGUAGE A first date

a) Read the text and fill in the correct forms of the words given or a suitable word.

Some things (1 change) since your parents (2 go)on their first date, — 1 ______ 2 ______

but lots of things are still the same. We asked our readers (3) advice they — 3 ______

would give others of the same sex (4 go) on a first date. Here are some of the answers: — 4 ______

The girls said:
Make sure you're going to do something both of you enjoy (5 do). For example, if your date suggests going to see a scary movie or going to a boxing match and you hate those things, suggest something else. — 5 ______
Don't be late.
Try to get to the meeting place (6) the time you agreed on. — 6 ______

Nobody likes (7 stand) around in the cold. — 7 ______

Dress (8 careful). Don't wear your oldest jeans with holes or shoes you — 8 ______

can't walk in. Don't talk (9) your ex-boyfriends. And don't agree (10) all your date's opinions. That's boring. — 9 ______ 10 ______

The boys said:
Be yourself, don't play a role. Don't try too hard to make a good — 11 ______

(11 impress). Don't talk about (12 you) too much. Don't (13) stupid jokes. — 12 ______ 13 ______

Show that you're a good listener. Don't talk about problems with your parents. Talk about music, concerts, films, famous people. Don't tell your date about your fantastic friends – she may be more interested in them (14) in you! — 14 ______

If your date isn't very (15 success), don't worry. Better luck next time! — 15 ______

b) Find words in the text that mean more or less the same.

1 like: ______ 2 put on: ______

3 views: ______ 4 part: ______

5 silly: ______ 6 well-known: ______

c) Find opposites in the text.

1 hate: ______ 2 exciting: ______

3 bored: ______ 4 different: ______

5 early: ______ 6 horrible: ______

d) Explain two of the following words in complete sentences.

1 scary: ______

2 advice: ______

3 opinion: ______

How did you do?

Check your answers to the Exam Check on p. 80. Then answer the questions below with yes or no. If you tick no or would like some extra practice on that point, go to the exercises in your workbook (▸ pp. 48–71).

1, 2, 3 LISTENING Friends on the net, Voicemail messages, Talking about …	Yes	No	Exercise
1 Konntest du nach dem 1. Hören beurteilen, um was es im Wesentlichen geht?	☐	☐	▸ 1–4
2 Hast du die Detailfragen ohne Probleme beantworten können?	☐	☐	▸ 4–8, 10, 11
3 Hast du Zahlen, Daten, Uhrzeiten, Telefonnummern usw. richtig verstanden?	☐	☐	▸ 5, 6
4 Konntest du den amerikanischen und australischen Akzent erkennen und verstehen?	☐	☐	▸ 7, 8
5 Konntest du dem Sprechtempo problemlos folgen?	☐	☐	▸ 9
4, 5, 6 SPEAKING Dumped, A cartoon, Comparing photos			
1 Hast du mit dem *present progressive* (z. B. *he is reading*) beschrieben, was die Personen auf den Bildern gerade tun?	☐	☐	▸ 30
2 Hast du wichtige Vokabeln für die Bildbeschreibung (z. B. *in the foreground* usw.) gewusst?	☐	☐	▸ 12
3 Hast du die Personen, ihre Gefühle und die Atmosphäre der Bilder mit passenden Adjektiven (z. B. *angry, happy, sad*) beschrieben?	☐	☐	▸ 33
4 Hast du problemlos Fragen bilden können und deine Meinung zu den Fragen ausdrücken können?	☐	☐	▸ 13, 14, 31
5 Hast du den Cartoon und die Aussage des Cartoon-Zeichners beschreiben können?	☐	☐	▸ 15
7 WRITING A questionnaire			
1 Hast du passende Vokabeln für eine Personenbeschreibung (z. B. *reliable, honest*) gewusst?	☐	☐	▸ 33
2 Hast du passende Vokabeln für Freizeit und Hobbys (z. B. *hang out, surf the net*) benutzt?	☐	☐	▸ 34
3 Hast du deine Rechtschreibung und Grammatik überprüft und deine Fehler korrigiert?	☐	☐	▸ 19
8 WRITING A picture story			
1 Hast du die *story* hauptsächlich im *simple past* und *past progressive* geschrieben?	☐	☐	▸ 32
2 Hast du passende Adjektive und Adverbien benutzt, um deine *story* auszuschmücken?	☐	☐	▸ 16
9 WRITING What's your opinion?			
1 Hast du deinen Text richtig strukturiert und mit Argumenten *dafür* und *dagegen* belegt?	☐	☐	▸ 14, 20
2 Hast du passende Satzadverbien (z. B. *However, First/Second, luckily*) als Übergänge für deine Argumente benutzt?	☐	☐	▸ 21
10 WRITING A report			
1 Hast du deine Ideen mithilfe eines *brainstorming* gesammelt und dazu Notizen gemacht?	☐	☐	▸ 18
2 Hast du die 5 Ws am Anfang deines Textes berücksichtigt?	☐	☐	▸ 22
3 Hast du für die Themen 1 und 3 das *simple past* und *past progressive* benutzt?	☐	☐	▸ 32
4 Hast du für die Beschreibung eines Films das *simple present* und *present progressive* benutzt?	☐	☐	▸ 30
5 Hast du linking words (*although, because, when, so, after*, etc.) benutzt?	☐	☐	▸ 17
11, 12 MEDIATION A letter to a problem page, Adverts			
1 Hast du beachtet, mit eigenen Worten nur das Wesentliche zusammenzufassen?	☐	☐	▸ 26–29
2 Hast du für unbekannte Wörter Umschreibungen benutzt (*paraphrasing*)?	☐	☐	▸ 35
13 READING Daniel's blog			
1 Konntest du schnell herausfinden, um was es in dem Text geht?	☐	☐	▸ 23a, 25a
2 Hast du nach Schlüsselwörtern (*key words*) gesucht, um Antworten zu finden?	☐	☐	▸ 25b
3 Hast du die Bedeutung unbekannter Wörter erschließen können?	☐	☐	▸ 24
14 USE OF LANGUAGE A first date			
1 Hast du fehlende Wörter aus *word families* richtig bilden können?	☐	☐	▸ 36
2 Hast du Gegensätze (*opposites*) im Text erkennen können?	☐	☐	▸ 37
3 Hast du englische Wörter/Begriffe auf Englisch erklären können (*paraphrasing*)?	☐	☐	▸ 35
4 Hast du fehlende Präpositionen richtig einsetzen können?	☐	☐	▸ 38

Unit 2 The world we live in

1 Modern gadgets ► p. 28

Read p. 28 of your student's book again. Write down as many examples of modern technology as you can think of, things that make your life easier and more fun. Make lists and compare them in class. Use a dictionary for words you don't know.

a) *Things that belong to me (or things I am allowed to borrow from my parents):*

mobile phone/smartphone, PC,

b) *Things used by all the family (kitchen, bathroom, etc.):*

TV, stereo,

c) *Choose three things from list a). Say what you use them for. How often do you need or use these things? For about how many hours a day do you need or use them? Write two sentences about each thing.*

1 Mobile phone: I use my mobile phone every day, ...

d) *Choose three things from list b). Say what your family needs them for and how often they are used. Write a few sentences.*

My sister and I use our DVD player quite a lot at the weekends. Mum uses ... Dad uses ...

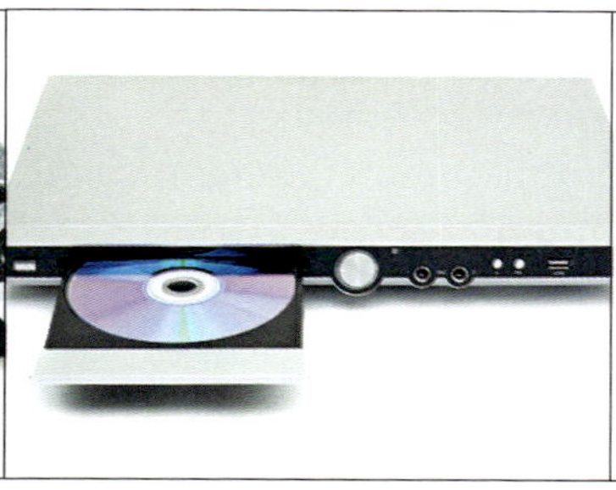

2201

2 LISTENING My family and our toys[1]

▸ p. 29 • WB (p. 72) 🎧 6

Test

Listen (🎧 6)[2] to what Trish says about her family's use of energy. Read the questions below first. Then answer them in a few words.

1 How many computers are there in Trish's family? ____________

2 Who's got a games console, a mobile and an MP3 player? ____________

3 Who's got an e-reader? ____________

4 Who uses social networking sites? ____________

5 Has Chris got a smart phone? ____________

6 Trish talks about some kitchen appliances. Which would you say is the most unnecessary?

____

7 Which appliances do they use in the bathroom? ____________

8 How many cars are there in the family? ____________

9 Are the cars petrol-driven or diesel? ____________

10 How do Trish and her brother get to school? ____________

WB, pp. 48–52

11 Who rides a bike? Where to? ____________

2302

12 Does anyone in the family care about trying to save energy? ____________

3 Ask Trish (Simple present: wh-questions)

▸ p. 29 🎧 6

Listen to what Trish says in exercise 2 (🎧 6) again. You want to know more about the family's use of energy. Write questions with question words: **when**, **where**, **what**, **why**, **how often**, **how long**, **how much/many**, *etc.*

1 *How many calls do you make on your mobile every day, Trish?*

2 *Why does your brother leave his computer on all night?*

3 ____________

4 ____________

5 ____________

6 ____________

7 ____________

8 ____________

9 ____________

2303

10 ____________

[1]toy [tɔɪ] *Spielzeug* [2]improve [ɪm'pruːv] *verbessern* juicer ['dʒuːsə] *Saftpresse* toothbrush ['tuːθbrʌʃ] *Zahnbürste* SatNav *Navigationsgerät* ('*Navi*')

4 REVISION Our carbon footprint (Passive: simple present)

▸ p. 32 • WB (p. 77)

Complete the text with verbs in the ***simple present passive****.*

A lot of energy _is needed_ (need) for all the machines and appliances that _are used_ (use) by each of us every day. Energy __________ (produce), for example, by burning oil and natural gas. But when these __________ (burn) CO_2 __________ (release) into the atmosphere. As more CO_2 __________ (send) into the atmosphere, more of the sun's heat __________ (trap[1]), so the earth's temperature rises.

The amount of CO_2 which __________ (produce) by each of us in one year __________ (call) our carbon footprint. In Germany 11 tonnes of CO_2 __________ (produce) by each person. CO_2 emissions __________ (cause) by almost everything we do, for example, when the TV or your computer __________ (turn on), when everyday kitchen appliances __________

2404 (use). But we can all help to reduce[2] emissions by saving energy, not wasting it.

5 REVISION How railways began (Passive: simple past)

▸ p. 32 • WB (p. 78)

Complete the sentences with suitable verbs from the box. Use each verb once in the ***simple past passive****.*

build • drive • improve[3] • ~~invent~~ • make • offer • put • use • win

In England the first steam engine _was invented_ by Thomas Newcomen in 1712, but because it was very big, it was not a very good machine. About 50 years later this engine __________ by James Watt, and soon his steam engines __________ in coal mines and factories throughout the north of England. Then a young man named George Stephenson had a very good idea. One of Watt's steam engines __________ on wheels and __________ to run on rails[4], pulling trucks[5] of coal behind it. After that, Stephenson thought that engines could also carry passengers and goods[6], so rich people began to build railways. In 1829 a prize __________ for the best locomotive engine, and the prize __________ by Stephenson for his *Rocket*. After that, railways __________ throughout the country, and soon ships __________ by steam instead of by wind.

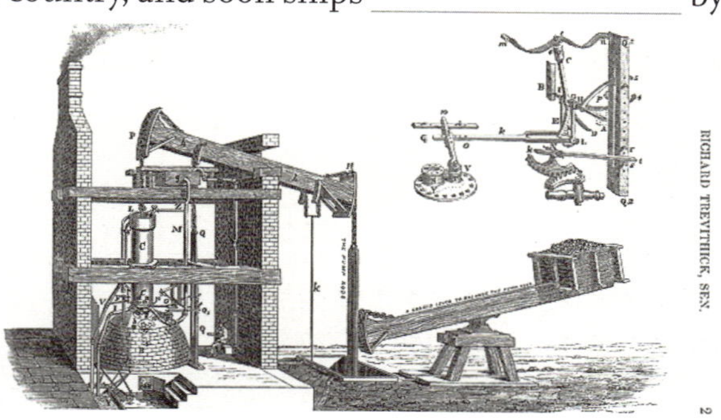

2405

[1]trap [træp] *einschließen, fangen* [2]reduce [rɪ'dju:s] *reduzieren* [3]improve [ɪm'pru:v] *verbessern* [4]rail *Schiene* [5]truck *kleiner Waggon* [6]goods [gʊdz] *Güter*

6 WORDS Inventors and their inventions ► p. 32

a) Complete the sentences with the inventions named on pp. 30–32 of your student's book.

1 Henry Ford's mass production of the *Model T* made it possible for almost everyone to afford a car.

2 The invention of the ______ was the first step towards the Industrial Revolution.

3 ______ made it fast and easy to send messages to people living far away.

4 Volta was an Italian physicist. His ______ allowed people to store electric power.

5 Invented by Wilhelm Röntgen, the ______ made it possible to see the bones inside the human body.

6 ______, discovered by Alexander Fleming, made it possible to save lives by fighting infectious disease.

b) When were they invented? Begin with the oldest invention. Write sentences with the words given.

steam engine/invent • Model T/build • X-ray machine/invent • penicillin/discover • electric battery/invent

1 *The steam engine was invented in 1712.*

2 ______

3 ______

4 ______

5 ______

7 Past and present (Simple present and simple past) ► p. 32 • WB (pp. 77–78)

*Complete the text with a suitable verb in the **simple present** or the **simple past**. You will need some of the verbs twice.*

arrive • find • *make* • phone • *ride* • send • talk • travel • write

Today we *make* journeys by car, train or plane, but in former times people *rode* horses to get from place to place, or they ______ by ship.

Before computers ______, people ______ letters and ______ them by post.

Now we ______ e-mails or text messages which ______ almost immediately.

In the past, people usually only ______ their friends at their home. Since the arrival of mobile phones, people ______ to friends almost anywhere at any time. Before the internet was born, you ______ information mainly in libraries. Now you can ______ information on the internet on any subject 24 hours a day.

2507

Now you

Talk to your parents and grandparents. Think of more things that are different today because of science and technology. Ideas: ask about dishwashers, digital watches, answering machines, videos, DVDs. Write a paragraph in your exercise book.

In the past people ... but now we ...

8 SPEAKING An important invention
▸ p. 32 • WB (pp. 74–75)

WB, pp. 53–55

*Do research about an inventor and his invention. If you wish, you can choose an inventor from exercise 6 of your workbook (p. 25). Use a library or the internet. Make notes and prepare to talk about your chosen invention in class for about three minutes. Use the **simple past active** and **passive**. Write in your exercise book.*

2608 *I'd like to talk about Henry Ford and his Model T. Ford built … It was sold for …*

9 WORDS The odd word out
▸ p. 32

Find the odd word out. Say how it is different.

1 CO_2 emissions • carbon dioxide • double glazing • climate change • carbon footprint

'Double glazing' is the odd word out because the others have to do with global warming.

2 antibiotics • infectious disease • penicillin • insulation • X-ray machine

3 Model T • steam engine • fossil fuel • Pilot ACE • X-ray machine

4 dishwasher • washing machine • microwave • solar energy • kettle

2609

10 MEDIATION Flight check-in service
▸ p. 33 • WB (p. 77)

Test

Your American exchange student is flying back to the US. Explain in English how she can check in for her flight without having to stand in a queue at the airport. Remember, report only the most important information. Make notes in your exercise book.

Mit unserem **FlyEasy e-Check-in** können Sie selbst entscheiden, wie und wann Sie für Ihren bevorstehenden Flug einchecken möchten. Am Flughafen können Sie sich viel Zeit ersparen, indem Sie Ihre Bordkarte[1] bequem zu Hause oder von unterwegs ausdrucken. Wenn Sie möchten, können wir Ihre Bordkarte auch auf Ihr Mobiltelefon senden. Um Ihr Gepäck einzuchecken, zeigen Sie Ihre Bordkarte einfach am Gepäckannahmeschalter[2] vor. Sie gehen dann direkt zum Gate ohne warten zu müssen.

FlyEasy Online-Check-in
Sie können bereits 22 Stunden vor Abflug Ihre Online-Bordkarte ausdrucken. Gehen Sie auf die Webseite *FlyEasy.com/onlinecheckin*. Geben Sie Ihren Namen, Buchungscode[3] oder Kreditkartennummer ein. Wählen Sie Ihren Sitzplatz aus. Drucken Sie Ihre Bordkarte aus. Ihr Gepäck geben Sie am Flughafen schnell und bequem an einem unserer Gepäckannahmeschalter auf.

FlyEasy Mobile Check-in
22 Stunden vor Abflug können Sie auch bequem von Ihrem Mobiltelefon aus einchecken. Rufen[4] Sie *FlyEasy.com* im Webbrowser auf und klicken Sie auf Check-in. Wie beim Online-Check-in geben Sie Ihren Namen, Buchungscode oder Kreditkartennummer ein. Wählen Sie dann Ihren Sitzplatz aus. Ihre Bordkarte wird kurz darauf direkt auf Ihr Mobiltelefon gesendet. Ihr Gepäck geben Sie am Flughafen schnell und bequem an einem unserer Gepäckannahmeschalter auf.

Wir wünschen Ihnen einen guten Flug!

WB, pp. 66–67

[1]boarding pass [2]baggage drop-off counter [3]booking code [4]go to

11 READING WORKING WITH THE TEXT Welcome to the future

▸ pp. 34–35

a) *Read pp. 34–35 of your student's book again. Match the sentence halves.*

1 The UK government introduces carbon rationing	• for two hours a day.
2 Children have to give up carbon points	• without their carbon rationing card.
3 People can't use buses	• to reduce Britain's carbon footprint.
4 Computers and television can only be used	• to help with the family energy allowance.
5 Laura and her mum had to get off the bus	• makes Laura feel scared.
6 Students pay for college heating with their cards	• because her mum couldn't find her carbon card.
7 Laura and her family	• but it's very cold anyway.
8 The cold, dark house	• don't spend time together any more.

b) *Explain how carbon rationing works.*

Carbon rationing gives each person an allowance of 200 carbon points a month.

c) *How does the carbon rationing system change the life of the Browns? Give examples from the text.*

The Browns' family life changes completely.

d) *Does the story make you think? Does it shock you or scare you? Do you think there are other ways of reducing the country's carbon footprint? Write down your opinion.*

The carbon rationing described in the story is very extreme. I think

/B, pp. 2–65

Extra Now you

How could you and your family save carbon points if you had to? Ideas: saving electricity, water, petrol, heating. Write notes in your exercise bock and discuss your answers in class.

I could use my ... less and I would remember to ... *I think my sister/brother could ...*

12 SPEAKING Describing a cartoon ▸ p. 36 • WB (pp. 74–75)

Test

Describe the cartoon. Make notes in your exercise book and discuss your answers in class. The following questions can help you.

1 What can you see in the picture (people and place)?

A boy is in the library. There's a woman ...

2 What is happening? Who is saying what?

The boy has read the sign. He is asking ...

3 What is the message? What does the cartoon artist want to say to the reader?

I think the cartoon artist wants to say/show that ...

4 Do you think the cartoon is easy to understand? Does it make you think about its message? Do you agree with the cartoon's message? Give examples to support your opinion.

WB, pp. 53–55

"Excuse me, but do you have any books?"

13 WORDS Helping the environment ▸ p. 36

a) Match.

Take	less water.
Heat	more trees.
Plant	shorter showers.
Eat	organic food.
Buy	electricity.
Don't waste	products with lots of packaging.
Don't buy	low-energy products.

b) Choose four things from a) above and write four sentences.

2813

We shouldn't buy products with lots of packaging because that causes unnecessary rubbish.

INFO BOX

More than 50% of schools in Britain are members of the *Eco-Schools International Environmental Programme.* Schools can win awards for 'green activities'. These are, for example, saving money spent on electricity, heating, water and rubbish collection in school. The highest award is the Green Flag[1] Award. Look up the website and see what you have to do: www.eco-schools-org.uk

[1]flag [flæg] *Fahne, Flagge*

14 Quiz: How green are you? ▸ p. 37

a) Read the questions and tick a box. Be honest! Work out your score at the bottom of the page.

1 How often do you buy pizza takeaways or fast food takeaways?

A often B sometimes C never

2 How do you buy cola or other soft drinks?

A in plastic bottles B in cans C in recyclable glass bottles

3 The television is on, but nobody is watching it. What do you do?

A leave it on B turn it off C leave it to others to decide

4 You're the last person to leave a room. Do you turn the lights off?

A always B sometimes C never

5 When you go shopping in a supermarket, do you ..?

A buy a plastic bag B reuse an old plastic bag C take a basket or a cloth[1] bag with you

6 What do you do with comics and magazines that you don't need any more?

A throw them away with the household rubbish B put them in a waste paper bin for recycling C give them to your friends, so it's their problem

7 When you clean your teeth, do you ...?

A turn the water on and off as you need it B leave the water running all the time C use just one glass of water

8 When the place where you're going isn't far, do you ...?

A walk or cycle B ask a parent to drive you C take a bus

9 Do you make unnecessary calls on your mobile?

A Yes, often. B No, I try not to. C Yes, sometimes.

10 On average, how many text messages do you send every day?

A under five B five to ten C more than ten

b) Count your points: ____________

1 A 0	B 1	C 2
2 A 0	B 0	C 2
3 A 0	B 2	C 1
4 A 2	B 1	C 0
5 A 0	B 1	C 2
6 A 0	B 2	C 0
7 A 1	B 0	C 2
8 A 2	B 0	C 1
9 A 0	B 2	C 1
10 A 2	B 1	C 0

20–15 points:	Well done! You behave intelligently and responsibly towards your environment. You try hard to save energy and water.
10–14 points:	You are going in the right direction[2], but you should still try harder.
Under 10 points:	Well, you still have a long way to go! Maybe you should think more seriously about environmental topics. Helping to save energy and water is not just for others.

[1]cloth [klɒθ] *Stoff* [2]direction [də'rekʃn] *Richtung*

15 WORDS 'Green' or 'non-green'? ▸ p. 37

a) Sort the words and phrases into 'green' and 'non-green'. Write two lists.

burn fossil fuels • chemicals • climate change • CO_2 emissions • destroy[1] forests • *double glazing* • global warming • insulation • low-energy products • organic farms • plant trees • plastic bags • pollution • recycle • reduce waste • solar energy • wave power • wind power

☺ *double glazing,* ______________________________

____

____

____

☹ *burn fossil fuels,* ______________________________

____

____

____

b) How do these teenagers try to save energy? Complete what they say with words and phrases from a) above, in the correct form where necessary.

1 We always buy ______________ ______________, like fluorescent[2] light bulbs, so we save energy that way.

2 Now we buy our food from ______________ ______________ because they don't use ______________ in food production.

3 I eat less meat now, because in some countries they ______________ to make room[3] for cattle ranches[4].

4 We should use more ______________. It's easily produced in hot countries where the sun always shines.

5 If people don't do more to stop ______________, ice at the poles will start to melt.

6 In our family we ______________ all our old newspapers, glass and plastic too.

7 We try to reduce ______________ by walking and cycling instead of taking the car.

8 People should stop ______________ ______________ like oil, coal.

9 I never buy ______________ in supermarkets. I always take my basket with me.

10 Our house has good ______________, and the windows have ______________ ______________ so we can keep all the rooms warm.

3015

[1]destroy [dɪˈstrɔɪ] *zerstören* [2]fluorescent [ˌflɔːˈresnt] *reflektierend* [3]make room *Platz schaffen* [4]cattle ranch [ˈkætl ræntʃ] *Rinderfarm*

16 Get it right! (Prepositions) ▸ p. 37

Complete the sentences with the correct prepositions. Use: ***about, at, by, for, into, of, on, without.***

1 Are you interested *in* ______ reading ______ the causes ______ climate change?

2 One cause is that burning fossil fuels releases CO_2 ______ the atmosphere.

3 However, not only industry and cars are responsible ______ carbon emissions.

4 The amount ______ CO_2 you produce every year is called your carbon footprint.

5 Life ______ modern gadgets wouldn't be very easy.

6 Modern kitchens are full ______ useful electric appliances.

7 How much does the average person spend ______ heat, food and travel per month?

8 We can help to slow down global warming ______ walking and cycling more.

9 Simple ways ______ saving energy and water are turning off lights and taps[1].

3116 10 Everybody can do something. Are you good ______ saving energy and reducing waste?

17 WRITING Making schools greener (A written discussion) ▸ p. 37 • SF (p. 148)

Think of arguments for and against the statement below and present them in a written discussion. Use your exercise book.

We can do more to make school greener.

- Brainstorm your ideas and write notes in your exercise book. For example: use recycled paper, make fewer photocopies, don't use throwaway plastic pens, turn off heating, lights, computers, electronic equipment when not necessary
- Order your ideas **for** and **against** the statement.
- Give reasons or examples to support your arguments.
- Write an outline in the following form:

1 **Introduction** (Say what you are writing about and why the topic is important.)
I'm going to discuss how we could make school greener. This topic is very important because …

2 **Arguments** (Write arguments **for** and **against** the statement.)
2.1 First argument (with example or reason; start a new paragraph for each point)
2.2 Second argument (with example or reason; start a new paragraph for each point)
2.3 …
On the one hand, … • A lot of people think that … • First, … • for example, sometimes … • One reason is that … • Another reason/example is that … • A good example of this is … • Second, … • Finally, … • On the other hand, … • Another argument is that …

3 Conclusion (sum up the arguments and give your own point of view)
To sum up, I think … • That's why … • In my opinion, it is clear that …

WB, pp. 56–61

3118
3119

TIP 1
It is often better to begin with the point of view which you don't support. For example, if you think students and teachers can make schools greener, first say why some people think they can't do it.

TIP 2
Use sentence adverbs to introduce your arguments:
actually, however, luckily, sadly, perhaps, of course, probably.

[1]tap [tæp] *Wasserhahn*

Unit 3 Have your say!

1 Teen issues ▸ pp. 46–47

a) Youth magazine 'Teen voice' asked 14- to 17-year-olds what kind of things they cared about or spent free time on. Read some of the answers.

I'm interested in the news and stuff. I think we need to know what's happening in our country, for example with new laws about education and jobs, because that's important for our future.

I like doing volunteer work. I'm in a church group that looks after old people who live alone. We visit them, do shopping for them, just talk to them. They're happy when we spend time with them.

I think that teenage violence is becoming a real problem, so many gangs that hang out, so much anti-social behaviour. Sometimes kids carry knives, even guns. You never really feel safe in some places, not even in the daytime.

I love nature. I'm in a group that does clean-up projects. I hate it when people throw rubbish in the woods, like car tyres[1] and even old sofas. You can't imagine what we find!

I care about our four-legged friends, so I work in a rescue[2] centre for lost and unwanted pets at the weekends. I feed them, clean their cages and take the dogs for walks. They are so excited when we give them some love and attention.

We have some kids in our class from Eastern Europe. My classmates don't talk to them because they say their dads take away jobs from our dads. But that isn't fair, and even if it was true, it isn't the kids' fault. I call it discrimination, and I find it stupid.

b) Who cares about what? Match what the teenagers said with the statements below. Write the names. There are two statements that do not match.

1 Beth is interested in the country's politics.

2 ________ helps at an animal shelter[3].

3 ________ is worried about climate change.

4 ________ likes working for the environment.

5 ________ likes to do social work in the community.

6 ________ cares about discrimination of foreign immigrants.

7 ________ cares about people losing their jobs.

8 ________ is worried about teenage crime.

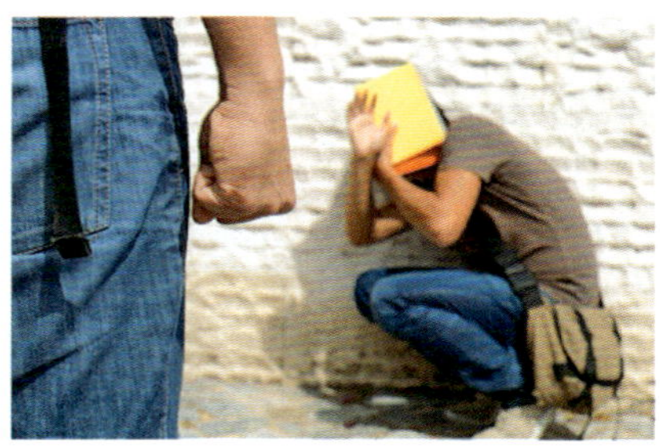

c) Which of the issues in a) and b) do you think are the most important? Name two and say why you think so. Which of the issues could you perhaps get interested in or involved with? Write in your exercise book.

3201 *I think ... is a very important issue for kids of my age group because ... If we don't ... the situation will get worse. What ... said is true for me too ...*

[1]tyre ['taɪə] *Reifen* [2]rescue ['reskjuː] *Rettung(s)-* [3]shelter ['ʃeltə] *Unterkunft, Asyl*

2 WORDS What you can do ▸ p. 47

Complete the text with words from the box in the correct form. You do not need all the words. Read the whole text carefully before you begin.

care • citizen • community • democracy • discrimination • environment • facilities • government • have your say • issue • law • MP • petition • rights • sign • stand up • support • town councillors • town hall

Young people have rights too. If something is happening that you don't agree with, then you should ______________ and try to change it. But do you ____________ enough to do anything about it? In our modern world there are many ____________ which are important for young people. Some problems are close to home, in your town or ______________. For example, maybe you think that young people in your neighbourhood need better or more ______________ for sports and free time. If lots of you think the same, you can ask people to ______________ you. You can create a ______________ and ask people to ____________ it. You can inform the local newspaper or radio station, go to the ______________ to talk to the ____________________. Somebody will listen. Other issues are important for your country, like social problems, education and jobs, ____________________ against minorities, making the ________________ clean and healthy. Many issues are important for people of all countries, like human rights, AIDS, drugs, global warming and preventing war. Young people can't solve the world's problems alone, but they can show that they care by ________________ and speaking out.

3302
3303

Extra Now you ▸ SF (pp. 125–126)

a) *Describe what you think is happening in the pictures. Write two short paragraphs in your exercise book.*

1

2

b) *What could young people in your school, neighbourhood, community or town do to improve[1] these bad situations? Make notes and discuss your ideas in class.*

[1]improve [ɪm'pruːv] *verbessern*

3 REVISION Which form? (Simple and progressive forms) ▸ p. 49 • WB (p. 77)

*Complete the sentences with the **simple** or the **progressive form** of the verb.*

1 At 16 young people in the UK *have* (have) the right to leave school.

2 My friend Joe *is thinking* (think) of leaving school in summer this year.

3 But he __________ (have) a hard time at home.

4 His parents __________ (think) he __________ (make) a big mistake.

5 They __________ (want) him to stay at school and do his exams because he __________ (do) well.

6 They __________ (believe) that having good exam results would give him a better chance of a good job.

7 Joe's parents __________ (not understand) why he __________ (seem) to dislike school.

8 But Joe __________ (not dislike) school, and he __________ (know) his parents are right.

9 It's just that at the moment he __________ (have) serious thoughts about the importance of exams.

3403 10 His cousin has a very good school-leaving certificate but he __________ (still, look) for a job.

4 REVISION Rights ▸ p. 49

Underline the correct preposition.

Oliver's article is (about/over) young people's rights. He says British teenagers (over/under) 18 have the right (to/of) be listened (at/to) and the right to meet (in/on) public. But shop owners only let teens enter a shop two (on/at) a time and (without/with) bags. When 16-year-olds go (in/to) the cinema, they pay adult prices, but (in/at) work 16-year-olds earn less than adults. They don't have the right (of/to) vote, although they can fight (in/with) the British army and pay taxes (of/to) the government. In Britain, four (from/out of/of) five 16-year-olds find all this unfair. But is their interest (in/for) politics strong enough to be able to vote responsibly?

3404

5 SPEAKING The mosquito ▸ p. 49 • WB (pp. 74–75)

Test

Prepare a two-minute talk about the mosquito.

1 Explain what it is to someone who has never heard about it.
2 Explain its possible advantages.
3 Explain its disadvantages.
4 Give your own opinion as a teenager about the mosquito.

WB, pp. 53–55

If you haven't heard of the mosquito, I'll begin by explaining what it is. It's a small device which …

6 READING A woman who stood up for women's rights

▸ p. 51 • WB (pp. 72–73)

Test

a) *Read the text about Emmeline Pankhurst, who fought for women's voting rights in Britain. Find suitable headings for the paragraphs. Write the letters A–F in the boxes. There is one more heading than you need.*

A A partner and supporter	B Failure	C Militant action
D The fight is over	E Slow beginnings	F Family background

☐ In Britain at the start of the 19th century only rich men were allowed to vote. People who were not rich also wanted voting rights, but Parliament said no. As a result people became angry and fighting broke out all over the country. Thousands demonstrated on the streets. Some were killed. Finally, in 1832 Parliament passed a law allowing more men to vote. Votes for women, however, were unthinkable.

☐ Even at the start of the 20th century women still did not have the vote. Some protested peacefully, but nothing changed. A woman called Emmeline Goulden, born in Manchester in 1858, also believed strongly that women should have voting rights. Her mother, a feminist, and her father, a businessman, had strong political views. As a young woman in the 1870s Emmeline went to feminist meetings with her mother. Emmeline was clever and loved reading, but because she was a girl she did not receive the same education as her five brothers. In those days a boy's education was more important.

☐ When Emmeline was 20, she married Dr Richard Pankhurst, a lawyer[1] who was 24 years older than her. He was a strong supporter of voting rights for women. Emmeline and her husband worked together on social projects, trying to improve the lives of the poor. Although Emmeline had five children in ten years, she never stopped working. Sadly, in 1898, Emmeline's husband suddenly became ill and died. She was left alone with her children, but she continued to work hard to help poor women living in workhouses[2], especially teenage mothers.

☐ In 1903 she founded the *Women's Social and Political Union*, together with her daughter Christabel, who was studying to become a lawyer. After a few years they realized that peaceful protest came to nothing and they were ready to fight for women's rights in a radical way. They disturbed[3] meetings in Parliament, they encouraged women to break the law by attacking police officers, breaking windows and setting fire to buildings. They did anything to draw the attention of the public and the law-makers to their cause[4]. Emmeline led protest marches and held speeches in the USA. In Britain Emmeline and Christabel were arrested[5] and put in prison many times. Many other members of the *WSPU* were arrested too. Some went on hunger strike in prison. Emmeline became seriously ill.

☐ When the First World War started in 1914, women still did not have the vote. However, Emmeline stopped all militant activities and encouraged women to support the government and work for their country. Many women did the work of men who were fighting in the war. When the war was over in 1918, women in Britain over the age of 30 and all men over the age of 21 were given voting rights. Ten years later in 1928 all women were at last given the same full voting rights as men. In the same year Emmeline Pankhurst died.

b) *Draw a timeline of the most important events in Emmeline Pankhurst's life. Use the* **simple present**. *Write in your exercise book.*

c) *In a few sentences, explain why she was important.*

d) *What do we learn from the text about Emmeline Pankhurst's character? Think about the social background at the time, her own family life and the work she did.*

WB, pp. 62–65

e) **Extra** *Do you agree with her methods[6]? Discuss this question in class.*

[1]lawyer ['lɔːjə] *Anwalt/Anwältin* [2]workhouse *Armenhaus* [3]disturb [dɪ'stɜːb] *stören* [4]cause [kɔːz] *Sache* [5]arrest [ə'rest] *verhaften* [6]method ['meθəd] *Methode*

7 LISTENING Young people and voting

▸ p. 51 • WB (p. 72) 7

Test

a) You are going to hear four UK students talking about voting. First read the statements in tasks a) and b). Then listen and tick the correct boxes.

1 The students talk about ...
- election promises. ☐
- the voting system in the UK. ☐
- why it's important to use your right to vote. ☐

2 Which students think voting is very important?
- The two girls. ☐
- One boy and one girl. ☐
- Just one girl. ☐

b) Write T (true) or F (false) after each statement while you are listening. Then listen again to check your answers.

1 Fran's sister is going to vote at the next election. .... F
2 Tom thinks that politicians make promises but they don't keep them. .... ☐
3 Mel believes that every vote counts. .... ☐
4 Syed thinks it's stupid to complain about how the country is run if you don't vote. .... ☐
5 Mel tells the other students about the history of women's votes in the UK. .... ☐
6 Tom thinks everyone should get involved with politics and voting. .... ☐
7 The first country to give women the vote was New Zealand. .... ☐
8 Women in Switzerland got the same voting rights as men in 1971. .... ☐
9 The voting age in Australia is 16. .... ☐
10 About 16% of young people in the UK have a job before they're 16. .... ☐

WB, pp. 48–52

3607

8 WRITING A letter to a teen magazine

▸ p. 51 • WB (pp. 75–76)

Test

Write a letter to a teen magazine. Say what you think is good and what is not so good about voting at 16. Would you vote if you could? Say why or why not. Write 100–120 words in your exercise book.

Dear mag,

I'd like to share my thoughts with other teenage readers on the topic of voting rights at 16.

In my opinion, ... Second, ... Another reason is that ...

On the other hand, a lot of 16-year-olds ...

My view is that ...

What do other readers who are under 18 think about voting at 16? ...

WB, pp. 56–61

9 WORDS What Oliver thinks ▸ p. 51

Choose and underline the correct word.

1 The mosquito is an anti-teenager (gadget/appliance/device).
2 Oliver says the mosquito is (amazing/surprising/disgusting).
3 Some signs on shop doors say 'No children (until/unless/although) with an adult.'
4 Other signs say 'Only 2 children (one by one/at a time/at any time).'
5 Teenagers often pay the same prices as adults. Oliver says that doesn't (make/give/mean) sense.
3709 6 Oliver thinks teenagers should take (part/place/action) to improve the situation.

10 REVISION Will CCTV be a good or a bad thing? (will/won't and conditional 1) ▸ p. 51 • WB (p. 79)

*Students in Bristol have heard that CCTV will be installed in their school in the holidays. Complete what the students say about it. Use **will**, **won't** and correct forms for **if**-clauses.*

1

I think it _will_ be a good thing. I think we _'ll_ behave better. For example, if troublemakers ________ (think) they are being watched, they ________ (leave) others alone. They ________ (vandalize) or bully. I'm for it.

2

I've read that exam results have improved a lot in schools with CCTV. Well, students ________ (try) to cheat[1] if they ________ (know) they're being watched, will they? So they learn – and pass!

3

CCTV will be good for security outside school hours. Thieves ________ (break in) and steal our computers and electronic equipment if they ________ (see) that there's CCTV in the building. I'm for it.

4

True. But then they ________ (bully) kids outside school. CCTV in school ________ (stop) bullying. And I think teachers should stop bullying, not cameras. I'm against it.

5

I think parents ________ (be) happy that their kids are safe in school. But ________ students be scared of giving wrong answers and expressing their ideas?

6

I'm sure the teachers ________ (watch) all the footage[2], but it's good to have proof on camera if it's needed. Kids who spray graffiti, damage[3] toilets or smoke ________ (be) found out. That's OK, isn't it? I'm for it too.

3710

INFO BOX

A school in Coventry, UK, is reported to have installed 112 CCTV cameras inside and outside the building. As the school has just over 1000 students, that means that there's a camera for every ten. The system is thought to improve[4] students' safety, to prevent break-ins and stealing. But even parents think that it's all too much. The school has been called 'Big Brother High'.

[1]cheat [tʃiːt] *täuschen* [2]footage ['fʊtɪdʒ] *Film(material)* [3]damage ['dæmɪdʒ] *beschädigen* [4]improve [ɪm'pruːv] *(sich) verbessern*

11 WORKING WITH THE TEXT Speaking out

▸ pp. 52–53

a) Read pp. 52–53 of your student's book again. Then put the sentences in the correct order. Write the numbers 2–9 in the boxes.

1 Mr Neck tells the class that his son can't get a job as a firefighter. ☐
2 David Petrakis stands up to protest against Mr Neck. ☐
3 Mr Neck says the USA should not have allowed immigrants into the country after 1900. ☐
4 In the History lesson Mr Neck writes the word 'immigration' on the board. 1
5 Mr Neck tells the class about his family history as American citizens. ☐
6 Lots of students put up their hands because they don't agree with Mr Neck. ☐
7 Mr Neck tells David to sit down and be quiet. ☐
8 David leaves the classroom in silent protest and earns Melinda's respect. ☐
9 Mr Neck closes the debate when one boy says something he doesn't want to hear. ☐

b) How would you assess Mr Neck's History lesson on a scale of 1 (very good) to 5 (very bad)? Explain your opinion. Look for lines in the text which support your views.

c) Look at what the 'brave kid' says in ll. 56–63. Why is he brave?

d) How do you think the situation between Mr Neck, the students of the History class and David Petrakis might continue? How might the next History lesson be?

e) Does this text extract make you want to read the whole novel Speak? Write down why or why not.

f) **Extra** *Use your notes from b)–e) to discuss your opinions in class.*

12 WORDS Word families ▸ p. 54

a) Complete the table with words from this unit.

VERB		NOUN	NOUN		ADJECTIVE
apologize	–	apology	______	–	different
______	–	concentration	______	–	intelligent
______	–	discrimination	______	–	polite
______	–	government	politician	–	______
immigrate	–	______	______	–	poor
speak	–	______	______	–	responsible
______	–	wish	______	–	true

b) Complete the sentences with words from a) in the correct form.

1 Do you think that politicians always tell the ______ ?

2 Do you think 16-year-olds have serious ______ views?

3 Voting for a party and what it stands for is a great ______ .

4 An important issue in the UK and in the USA is child ______ .

5 Are most people for or against more ______ into Britain?

6 It is illegal to ______ people because of their race, religion, age or sex.

7 In the novel *Speak* David Petrakis holds a short ______ about the rights of all citizens under the US Constitution.

8 Mr Neck and David have strong ______ of opinion on the subject of immigration.

9 Mr Neck behaves unfairly. Do you think he will offer David Petrakis an ______ ?

3912 10 If you had three ______ for the future, what would they be?

13 WORDS Which is correct? ▸ p. 54

Underline the correct word from the brackets.

1 Young people often (care about/wish for/concentrate on) child poverty.

2 You can show your support by (creating/signing/writing) a petition.

3 In the History class Mr Neck wanted to have a (decision/debate/announcement) about US immigration.

3913 4 David Petrakis said that free speech was a (question/issue/right) under the Constitution.

14 READING Iqbal's story ▸ p. 54 • WB (pp. 72–73)

Test

Read the story of Iqbal and complete the tasks below in your exercise book.

The story of a child hero

Iqbal Masih was born in a village in Pakistan in 1982. His parents did not have enough money to support the family, so when Iqbal was four, they sold him to a rich carpet[1]-maker for six years – for $200. The small child had to work 14 hours a day making carpets, in terrible conditions with little food. He worked together with many other children.

At the age of ten he was freed[2] by the *Bonded Labour Liberation Front*[3], an organization in Pakistan working against child labour[4]. Iqbal went to one of the organization's schools, with other children who had been child slaves. He was highly intelligent, so he learned well. He was brave too and wanted to help to free other child workers. He joined the organization as an international spokesman[5] for the millions of child workers in Pakistan. In Europe and America he spoke out against the cruel carpet trade, making the terrible conditions of child labour known. He also asked people to boycott carpets from Pakistani companies that used child labour. He was successful, the world listened. People stopped buying carpets made in Pakistan. Sales[6] fell heavily for three years, and Iqbal made many enemies in the carpet industry.

In 1994 Iqbal won the *Reebok Youth in Action Award* and he became known internationally as a child rights activist. Iqbal wanted to study in the USA and become a lawyer[7]. Brandeis University near Boston promised him a place after he had finished his school in Pakistan. But Iqbal had no future. In April 1995, at the age of thirteen, he was shot dead. His death was officially reported as an accident. There are different versions of why he was killed and who killed him.

UNICEF believes that about 90% of the Pakistani carpet industry uses child workers. Although buying children for child labour has been illegal in Pakistan since 1992, it still continues – and the law-breakers are not punished.

1 Summarize the text in five to six sentences.
2 Write words and phrases from the text which describe Iqbal.
3 How did you feel when you read this story? Shocked? Angry? Sad? Write a few sentences.
4 Why are there different versions of why he was killed and who killed him?
5 **Extra** There are many organizations which are working against child labour. Why is their work difficult? Make notes and discuss your thoughts in class.

WB, pp. 62–65

[1]carpet ['kɑːpɪt] *Teppich* [2]free *befreien* [3]BLLF *Front gegen die Schuldknechtschaft* [4]child labour ['leɪbə] *Kinderarbeit* [5]spokesman ['spəʊksmən] *Sprecher* [6]sales [seɪlz] *Umsatz* [7]lawyer ['lɔːjə] *Rechtsanwalt/-wältin*

15 EVERYDAY ENGLISH SPEAKING Conflicts

▸ p. 55 • WB (pp. 74–75) 8

a) *Which of the phrases below would you use to express the following? Write a number in the box. What should you not say? Write an 'X' in the box.*

1 start a conversation | 2 name a problem | 3 disagree that there is a problem | 4 apologize | 5 accept an apology

[4] I'm sorry. I didn't mean to ...	[ ] My mistake. I'm sorry.	[ ] Mind your own business.
[ ] Excuse me, but ...	[ ] The problem is ...	[ ] Where's the problem?
[X] Shut up.	[ ] Don't worry about it.	[ ] Sorry, but I don't see it that way.
[ ] Can I have a word with you?	[ ] OK. No worries.	[ ] It annoys me that ...
[ ] Sorry, I shouldn't have said ...	[ ] I don't see what's wrong with ...	

WB, pp. 53–55

b) *Listen to six people on your CD (8)[1]. React to what you hear, using one or more of the sentences above and/or your own sentence. Look at the example.*

1 (On a bus): You're staring[2] at me. Is there a reason for that?

4115

Oh, sorry. I didn't mean to stare at you. I was thinking of something else.

16 EVERYDAY ENGLISH MEDIATION Rules on alcohol in the UK

▸ p. 55 • WB (p. 77)

Test

a) *If you are on holiday or on a student exchange in the UK, it is important to know what you can and can't do. For example, when and where you are allowed to drink alcohol or to smoke. You have found some information on the internet. Make notes in German so that you can tell your friends. Keep your sentences simple. Don't translate. Write in your exercise book.*

Most countries have their own rules about when teenagers can drink what, and where they can drink it. The rules are not always simple.

Alcohol in the UK

In the UK, if you are under 16, you are not allowed to enter a pub, a bar or a place where alcohol is sold or drunk. However, if you are with an adult, you can go into most pubs, but you cannot have alcoholic drinks. If you are 16 or 17, you are allowed to drink wine or beer in a pub or restaurant, but only if you are with an adult who orders it with a meal. In Scotland, if you are 16 or 17, you can order wine or beer in a pub with a meal, but you needn't be with an adult.

You are not allowed to drink spirits[3] in pubs even with a meal until you are 18.

You also have to be 18 to buy and drink spirits in a bar or a pub and to buy spirits in a shop or supermarket. Mostly you will be asked to show your ID. It is illegal to buy alcohol for others who are under 18.

The rules for the minimum drinking age in the UK are not as strict as the rules in the USA.

WB, pp. 66–67

b) *Read p. 55 of your student's book again about the rules on alcohol in the USA. Compare them with the rules in the UK. Write three sentences with comparisons.*

4117 4118

To buy and drink alcohol you have to be older in the USA than in the UK.

[1]seat [siːt] *Sitz* jump the queue *vordrängeln* [2]stare [steə] *anstarren* [3]spirits ['spɪrɪts] *Spirituosen*

English for jobs

1 Confirming[1] an appointment ▸ p. 66 • WB (p. 74)

a) *Lena has applied to do an apprenticeship at a UK fashion company in Hamburg. She has received a letter inviting her to an interview with Mr Jerome Hill. She calls the company to confirm the date and time of the interview. What should Lena say? Tick A or B.*

Sandra *Fashions 21*, Sandra Moss speaking. How can I help you, please?
Lena A Good morning. I'm calling to confirm an interview with Mr Hill.
B I want to speak to Jerome Hill, please.

Sandra I see. May I ask who's calling, please?
Lena A Lena Hartmann.
B Yes, this is Lena Hartmann.

Sandra Just a moment please, Ms Hartmann. I'll put you through to Mr Hill's assistant.
Lena A Thank you.
B OK.

Sandra I'm sorry to keep you waiting, but nobody's answering. Would you like to hold?
Lena A No.
B Erm ..., no, thank you. It's OK. I'll try again later.

Sandra Would you like to leave a message?
Lena A Well, yes, if you don't mind. Would you please tell Mr Hill or his assistant that I'll be pleased[2] to come for interview on Friday at ten thirty?
B Yeah. Why not. Tell Mr Hill I'll be there on Friday at ten thirty. OK?

Sandra So that's Ms Hartmann for interview with Mr Hill on Friday at ten thirty. I'll pass on your message as soon as possible.
Lena A Thanks a lot. Goodbye.
B OK. See you.

Sanda You're welcome. Goodbye.

b) *Use phrases from a) above to write the following sentences in English.*

1 Ich möchte bitte einen Termin mit Mr Hill bestätigen.
I'd like to confirm an appointment with Mr Hill, please.

2 Wer spricht, bitte? ______

3 Moment, bitte. Ich verbinde. ______

4 Niemand geht ran. ______

5 Möchten Sie dran bleiben? ______

6 Danke. Ich versuche es später noch mal. ______

7 Möchten Sie eine Nachricht hinterlassen? ______

8 Würden Sie bitte Mr Hill ausrichten, dass ... ______

9 Ich gebe Ihre Nachricht so bald wie möglich weiter. ______

4201 10 Gern geschehen. ______

[1]confirm [kən'fɜːm] *bestätigen* [2]be pleased [pliːzd] *sich freuen*

2 Preparing for an interview

▸ p. 67 • WB (p. 74)

a) *Anton Schneider has applied to do an apprenticeship (AE= internship) with Amcom, a US computer company in Berlin. To prepare for his interview in English he is making notes on what he might say and ask. Not all his ideas are good. Tick (✔) the statements and questions which you think are suitable and cross (✘) the ones which are not.*

1 Would I have my own computer and telephone? ✘
2 My everyday English is quite good, and I'd love the chance to improve it. ✔
3 What exactly would I learn about the computer business? ☐
4 Would I have to make coffee for everybody? ☐
5 I've looked at the company's website, so I already have a lot of general information. ☐
6 I did work experience in an office last summer, and I didn't like it at all. The boss was really unfriendly. ☐
7 Which departments[1] would I work in? ☐
8 Would I have to work late because I go to sport three times a week? ☐
9 I'm really interested in computers and I'd be very excited about working here. ☐
10 Is the pay good? ☐
11 I'd like to work for your company because I want to learn all I can about the computer business. ☐
12 I like meeting new people and I love travelling. ☐
13 Who would be my boss? ☐
14 These offices are much more modern than the last place I worked in. ☐
15 What would my working hours be? ☐
16 I'm a brilliant team leader. ☐
17 People say that I'm well organized and reliable. And I work hard. ☐
18 How long are the coffee breaks and how many do we get? ☐
19 I'm willing[2] to work evenings or Saturdays if that's necessary. ☐
20 I'd be brilliant with US visitors. I have lots of American friends on Facebook. ☐

b) *How would you answer the following interview questions? Think carefully, then write Anton's answers.*

1 Can you tell me more about why you'd like to work for us?

2 Tell me something about your strengths. What do you like doing and what are you good at?
Ideas: ***very interested in ..., reliable, hard-working, motivated, good at organizing ...***

4302

[1]department [dɪ'pa:tmənt] *Abteilung* [2]willing ['wɪlɪŋ] *bereit, gewillt*

3 Arriving for an interview

► p. 67 • WB (p. 74) 9

a) Lena has just arrived for her interview and is talking to the receptionist. First, write who says what with R (receptionist) and L (Lena). Then put the dialogue in the right order and write it out in your exercise book.

- Right, Ms Hartmann. I'll let Mr Hill know that you've arrived. Erm, ...would you like to sign the visitors' book, please? ______
- No, thank you. I'll just wait here. ______
- Just here on the right. ______
- Good morning. Can I help you? 1, R
- Oh, good. Thank you. ______
- Could I have your name, please? ______
- Yes, of course. Where do I sign? ______
- Good morning. I have an interview with Mr Hill at ten thirty. 2, L
- I'm afraid Mr Hill isn't answering, but I'll call his assistant. Would you like to sit over there while you're waiting? ______
- Yes, it's Hartmann, Lena Hartmann. ______
- OK. Mr Hill is expecting you now. His assistant will be here in a moment to take you up. ______
- You're welcome. ______

b) Listen to your CD (9) and check that you have the correct order.

c) Find at least three phrases in the dialogue that are typical of polite English. Write them down with their German translations.

______

______

______

4403 ______

4 Polite small talk

► p. 69 • WB (p. 74)

Jane, Mr Hill's assistant, meets Lena at the reception. On the way up in the lift, Jane makes friendly conversation with Lena. Use the notes to write a suitable dialogue in English in your exercise book.

- Jane introduces herself to Lena.
- Lena tells Jane who she is.
- Jane asks Lena to follow her to the lifts. She tells her that they are going up to the fourth floor.
- Jane asks Lena if she found the way easily.
- Lena answers that it was no problem. The journey by bus took only half an hour.
- Lena asks Jane if other candidates are being interviewed.
- Jane tells Lena that she is the only applicant[1] today.
- On the fourth floor Jane shows Lena where Mr Hill's office is and asks her to take a seat[2] outside.
- Jane says that Mr Hill will be ready to see her in a few minutes.
- Lena thanks Jane.

4404 Jane *Hello, my name's Jane Kelly. I'm Mr Hill's assistant ...*

[1]applicant ['æplɪkənt] *Bewerber/in* [2]take a sit [siːt] *Platz nehmen*

5 An interview

► p. 69 • WB (p. 74) 10, 11

a) Mr Hill introduces himself and asks Lena into his office. Take Lena's role and answer Mr Hill's questions. You can make notes first, then listen (10) and speak in the pauses. Don't answer with only yes or no. Use polite phrases and small talk where suitable.

Mr Hill Hello, Lena. My name's Jerome Hill. Please take a seat.

Lena ______

Mr Hill Did you find the way here easily?

Lena ______

Mr Hill Would you like you some tea or coffee? Or water perhaps?

Lena (says no politely) ______

Mr Hill Well, thank you for your interest in our company. You sent us a letter of motivation, so perhaps you could tell me why you'd like to do your apprenticeship with us. Are we special in any way?

Lena ______

______

Mr Hill I see. Well, that sounds fine. Perhaps you could tell me a little about your strengths. Why should we choose you?

Lena ______

______

______

______

______

______

Mr Hill Good. Now what about school, Lena. How are your grades? Is your written English as good as your spoken English?

Lena ______

Mr Hill That's what you'd need most here. At least fifty per cent of the people who work here are from the UK, and we have lots of visitors from the UK. Sometimes from the USA too. How would you feel about looking after them, maybe telling them about Hamburg, that sort of thing?

Lena ______

Mr Hill OK. Now tell me, Lena. When could you start if we offered you an apprenticeship?

Lena ______

Mr Hill Well, Lena, I think that's all for today. Thank you for coming. We'll be in contact with you early next week. Oh, and about the reference you mentioned. Could you send it to us as soon as possible?

4505 *b) Listen (11) to the complete interview with Lena's answers. Check that you had something similar.*

6 A thank-you letter ▸ p. 69 • SF (p. 146)

a) After an interview it is often a good idea to write a short thank-you letter to the interviewer. Lena's English teacher gives her this advice:

- Thank Mr Hill for inviting you to the interview yesterday.
- Say that you appreciate the time he spent with you.
- Say that you enjoyed meeting him and his assistant.
- Say you were impressed by the friendly atmosphere in the company.
- Confirm your interest in working for *Fashion 21*.
- Say when you would be available to start work.
- Give the name and telephone number of a person to contact for a reference.
- Say that you look forward to hearing from him soon.

Write the main part and the end of Lena's letter. If you write the letter on your computer, see p. 146 of your student's book for help with formal letters.

…
Dear Mr Hill

I am writing to ____________________

____

____

____

____

____

Please contact Mr Johannsen for a reference:
H. Klaus Johannsen, Alster Wohndesign, Tel. (040) 73983145.

____

____

4606

7 Phone calls on the job ▸ p. 70 • WB (p. 72) 12

Listen to five short phone calls (12). Match the calls with the descriptions below. There are two descriptions which don't match any call. Write the number of the call (1–5) in the correct box.

Der Anrufer/Die Anruferin …

- möchte sich für einen Fehler entschuldigen. ☐
- möchte ein Datum für ein Treffen festlegen. ☐
- möchte seine Ankunftszeit mitteilen. ☐
- möchte die Gesprächspartnerin zum Essen einladen. ☐
- möchte mit jemandem sprechen, der zurzeit in einer Besprechung ist. ☐
- möchte eine Bestellung aufgeben. ☐
- möchte zurückgerufen werden. ☐

4607

8 Looking after visitors ▸ p. 70

a) Anton is now working at Amcom in Berlin. Today it's his job to welcome a US visitor, who has just arrived at reception. Which of the following could Anton use? Tick (✔) or cross (✘) the speech bubbles.

- How's the weather in New York? I expect it's warmer than here! ☐
- Did you have a good flight? ✔
- You look tired. Didn't you sleep on the plane? ☐
- Welcome to *Amcom*. My name's Anton Schneider, but please call me Toni. ☐
- Is this your first visit to Berlin? ☐
- Hello, you must be Ms Wilson. Pleased to meet you. ☐
- Our cafeteria on the top floor serves excellent coffee. There's also a great view of the city from up there too. May I suggest that we start there? ☐
- We can have a light lunch in our cafeteria. It's not very good, but it's cheap. ☐
- Mr Schmidt would like me to show you round. If you'd like that, I'd be happy to introduce you to a few people. ☐
- Mr Schmidt asked me to show you round, but there isn't much to see, I'm afraid. ☐
- It's my job to look after you this morning, until the meeting starts at 2 pm. ☐

4708 *b) Write a short dialogue between Anton and Ms Wilson. Use the phrases you ticked (✔) in a suitable order. Write in your exercise book.*

9 Saying goodbye ▸ p. 70 • WB (p. 74) 🎧 13

After the conference, Anton says goodbye to the visitor from New York. He is polite and friendly. Choose suitable phrases from the box to complete the dialogue. Then check with your CD (🎧 13).

> *I see you're ready to leave us now.* • Would you like me to call you a cab to the airport? • And I hope you had time to do some sightseeing. • I hope you had a good meeting. • It was nice meeting you. Have a good flight. • OK, so your cab will be there in a few minutes.

Anton	Hello again, Ms Wilson. *I see you're ready to leave us now.*
Ms Wilson	Yes, that's right. I'm flying back to the States this evening.
Anton	______________________
Ms Wilson	Yes, we did. Successful and enjoyable, thank you.
Anton	______________________
Ms Wilson	Well, I didn't have time for the city tour, but, well, next time maybe.
Anton	______________________
Ms Wilson	Oh, yes, thank you. That would be great.
Anton	______________________
Ms Wison	Thank you, Toni. See you again next year, maybe.
Anton	Goodbye. ______________________

4709

LISTENING

In this part of your workbook you will find exercises that will help you prepare for exams.

1 Holidays (Listening for gist) ▸ WB (p. 72) 14

Look at the pictures. Then listen to five students talking about the kind of holidays they like. Match the speakers to the pictures. Write the speaker numbers (1–5) in the boxes.

2 Talking about problems (Listening for gist) ▸ WB (p. 72) 15

Listen to four teenagers talking about their problems. Who is talking about what? Match the number of the speaker to the problem. There is one more than you need.

- Speaker 1 …
- Speaker 2 …
- Speaker 3 …
- Speaker 4 …

- wants to dump a friend.
- heard a friend tell lies[1].
- knows that someone fancies her boyfriend.
- is bad at school and can't tell his dad.
- needs money back that a friend borrowed.

3 Computer talk (Listening for gist) ▸ WB (p. 00) 16

Listen to four teenagers. What are they talking about? Write a letter (A–D) after each name below.

A Blogging	B Help chat rooms
C Social networking	D Skyping

4803
4804

1 Josh ☐ *2* Sarah ☐ *3* Mike ☐ *4* Ellie ☐

Tip

Think about words you need to talk about the topics A–D.
Then listen for them. For example:
blogging > *diary, update, read*
help chat rooms > *problem*
social networking > *friends, log on*
skyping > *phone, video, webcam*

[1]lie [laɪ] *Lüge*

4 Shopping (Listening for gist and detail) ▸ *WB (p. 72)* 17

a) *Listen to two US teenagers, Beth and Amy. Where do you think they are? Tick the correct box.*

At a street market. ☐ In a department store. ☐ In a shoe shop. ☐

b) *Listen again. What did the girls buy? Tick the correct box.*

- A top and a pair of black jeans. ☐
- Two tops and a pair of white jeans. ☐
- Two tops and a pair of blue shorts. ☐

4904

Tip

When listening to informal speech (especially AE), expect to hear shortened forms, missing verbs and grammatically incorrect verb forms, such as ***gonna*** (*going to*), ***wanna*** (*want to*), ***dunno*** (*don't know*), ***gotta*** (*have got to*), ***kinda*** (*kind of*).

5 Numbers, times, dates, letters (Listening for detail) ▸ *WB (p. 72)* 18–21

a) *You are going to hear numbers, dates and telephone numbers spoken quickly. Listen (18) and mark what you hear: one of each pair.*

14 / 40	15 / 50	160 / 116	347 / 374
1945 / 1954	2018 / 2080	0145500341 / 0144500341	06625330 / 06629330

b) *Listen (19) and write the numbers, dates and telephone numbers (in figures, not words: e.g. 175).*

1 16 ______ *5* ______

2 ______ *6* ______

3 ______ *7* ______

4 ______ *8* ______

Tip

1 Differentiate between the endings '-y' and '-een': e.g. *70* and *17*.

2 Numbers and years are spoken differently:
- 1984 (**number**): one thousand nine hundred and eighty-four.
- 1984 (**year**): nineteen eighty-four.

c) *Listen (20) and write the time in figures (e.g.: 10.30).*

1 ______ *2* ______ *3* ______ *4* ______

d) *Which letters of the alphabet do you hear (21)?*

4905 *1* ______ *2* ______ *3* ______ *4* ______ *5* ______ *6* ______

6 Announcements (Listening for detail) ▸ *WB (p. 72)* 22

Listen to the airport announcements and tick the correct box.

	True	False	Not given
1 Flight PS502 to Kiev has been cancelled[1] because of bad weather.	☐	☐	☐
2 The gate number has been changed for passengers to Glasgow.	☐	☐	☐
3 The flight number for the Glasgow flight is BE2958.	☐	☐	☐
4 The flight to Glasgow is delayed[2].	☐	☐	☐
5 The flight to the Isle of Man is boarding[3] at Gate 30.	☐	☐	☐
6 There is a 50-minute delay on the flight to Chicago.	☐	☐	☐
7 The flight to Budapest will leave as scheduled.	☐	☐	☐
8 The Budapest flight will depart from Gate 23.	☐	☐	☐
9 The flight to Toronto will depart at half past twelve.	☐	☐	☐
10 The Toronto flight is delayed by about 45 minutes.	☐	☐	☐

4906

[1]cancelled ['kænsəld] *gestrichen* [2]delayed [d'leɪd] *verspätet* [3]board [bɔːd] *einsteigen*

7 Where are they from? (Accents) ▸ WB (p. 72) 🎧 23

Listen to six teenagers talking about sightseeing in London. Are they British, American or Australian? Write UK, US or Australia under the pictures.

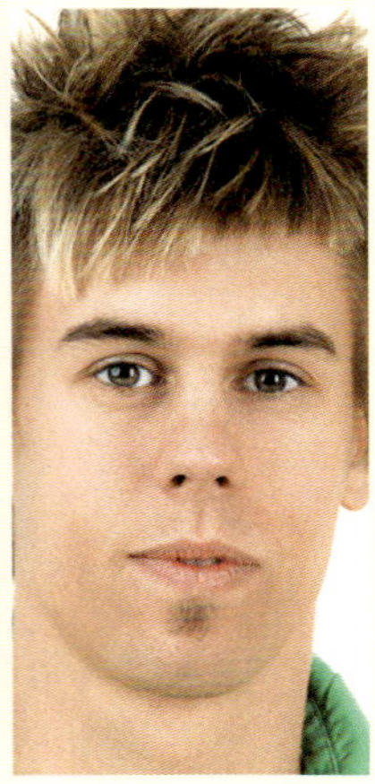

5007

1 ______ 2 ______ 3 ______ 4 ______ 5 ______ 6 ______

8 AE and BE ▸ WB (p. 72) 🎧 24

Listen to the US words and write down the British words.

5008

1 film
2 ______
3 ______
4 ______
5 ______
6 ______
7 ______
8 ______
9 ______
10 ______
11 ______
12 ______
13 ______
14 ______
15 ______
16 ______
17 ______
18 ______

9 A first job (Fast speech) ▸ WB (p. 72) 🎧 25

a) Listen to Mike and Terry talking about Terry's job. What do they talk about? Tick the correct boxes.

A The working hours. B The pay.
C The boss. D The kind of work.

b) What does Terry do at work? Tick the correct boxes.

A Serve petrol. B Take money.
C Serve customers. D Fill[1] the shelves.
E Clean the toilet. F Answer the phone.

5009

Tip

Compare the main pronunciation differences of BE and AE:

	BE	AE
last, ask	[ɑː]	[æ]
clock, hot	[ɒ]	[ʌ]
new, Tuesday	[juː]	[uː]
here, shirt, park >	In AE you hear the 'r'.	
city, better, writer >	In AE 't' in the middle of a word sounds like 'd'.	

[1]fill [fɪl] *(auf)füllen*

c) Are the following statements true or false? Tick the correct box.

	True	False	Not given
1 Terry works on Saturdays and Sundays.	☐	☐	☐
2 He works at a self-service petrol station.	☐	☐	☐
3 He had worked at a supermarket check-out before.	☐	☐	☐
4 There are lots of phone calls from customers on Saturdays.	☐	☐	☐
5 His shift is eight hours long.	☐	☐	☐
6 Three assistants work in the shop for each shift.	☐	☐	☐
7 Terry doesn't like Alice and Barry very much.	☐	☐	☐
8 He gets paid more than the standard rate[1].	☐	☐	☐
9 Terry is sixteen years old.	☐	☐	☐
10 The assistants pay the same prices as the customers.	☐	☐	☐

10 A radio phone-in (Listening for detail) ▸ *WB (p. 72)* 26

You are going to hear a radio phone-in about young people and their families. Read the tasks below, then listen and tick the correct answer: A, B or C.

Tip

With **multiple-choice tasks** it is often best to read the answers carefully before you listen, so you know what to listen for. If you are not sure the first time, write '?', then concentrate on the missing answers when you listen again.

1 The phone-in is about …
- A divorced people.
- B single-parent families.
- C patchwork families.

2 Mark lives with …
- A his stepdad.
- B his dad.
- C his mum and his sister in Scotland.

3 Jan is …
- A Mark's stepsister.
- B Mark's mother.
- C Mark's sister.

4 Marie has got …
- A one stepsister and one stepbrother.
- B two stepbrothers and a stepsister.
- C three stepbrothers.

5 Sharon is …
- A Marie's stepmother.
- B Marie's stepsister.
- C Marie's mum.

6 David's dad lives in …
- A London.
- B Sydney.
- C San Francisco.

7 David is from …
- A the UK.
- B the USA.
- C Australia.

8 David lives …
- A with his father and stepmother.
- B with his mother and stepfather.
- C in Sydney.

9 Nicole's dad lives in …
- A Coventry.
- B Oxford.
- C France.

10 Nicole has got …
- A a stepsister in France.
- B a stepbrother in France.
- C a brother in France.

[1]rate [reɪt] *Satz*

11 Teen work and pay in the UK (Listening for detail) ▸ WB (p. 72) 27

a) Read the tasks before you listen. Then listen and tick the correct box(es) to complete the sentences. Sometimes two of three boxes are correct. Check your answers when you listen a second time.

1 If you're 13,	☐ you can work for two hours on school days. ☐ you can work in a factory. ☐ you can work for two hours before school.
2 If you're 14,	☐ you can work 12 hours a week during term time. ☐ you can do all kinds of work. ☐ you can't work in a factory.
3 In the school holidays, if you're 13 or 14,	☐ you can work 5 hours on weekdays and Saturdays. ☐ you are allowed to work 25 hours a week altogether. ☐ you aren't allowed to work on Sundays.
4 In the school holidays, if you're 15 or 16,	☐ you can work 35 hours a week. ☐ you can work all day on Sundays. ☐ you can work between 10 pm and 6 am.
5 The National Minimum Wage[1] for 16- and 17-year-olds is	☐ £ 3.64 an hour. ☐ £ 4.92 an hour. ☐ no fixed rate[2].

b) Listen again and answer the questions in note form.

1 What is the name of the radio programme? ______

2 What is the programme about today? ______

3 What is the school-leaving age in the UK? ______

4 What kind of work are 13-year-olds allowed to do? ______

5 How many hours a day can you work at age 13? ______

6 How many hours a week can you work at age 14? ______

7 How many hours can you work on Saturdays at 14? ______

8 How many hours can 15- and 16-year-olds work on Saturdays? ______

9 You have to be ... to get the National Minimum Wage. ______

10 How many hours a week can 13–14-year-olds work in the holidays? ______

11 How many hours a day can 13–16-year-olds work on Sundays? ______

12 How much is the NMW if you are aged 18–20? ______

Tip

Look for **key words** in the tasks and mark them.
Numbers are always important, so listen carefully. Listen exactly for similar phrases e.g. *hours a day* or *hours a week*.

[1]National Minimum Wage [weɪdʒ] *gesetzlicher Mindestlohn* [2]fixed rate [ˈfɪkst ˌreɪt] *fester Satz*

SPEAKING

12 Describing pictures

▸ *SF (pp. 125–126)* • *WB (pp. 74–75)* 🎧 28

a) *Look carefully at the picture. Brainstorm vocabulary you need to describe the scene: action, people, background, atmosphere. Make notes below. If you don't know the words you need, look them up in a dictionary. Prepare to speak for about two minutes.*

Scene: *school sports day, end of school year,* ____________________

____

People, actions: *visitors, parents,* ____________________

____

Atmosphere, feelings: *ambitious,* ____________________

____

b) *Describe the picture using your vocabulary from a). Speak clearly and not too fast.*

- Describe the scene, where it is, what is happening.
  The picture shows a scene in summer. I think the picture was taken in/at …
- Describe the people. What are they doing/wearing, what are they probably speaking about? Use the following: ***on the right/left, in the middle/centre/ background/foreground, at the top/bottom of the picture, at the front/back, behind, in front of, over, under, on, next to, between.***
  The people seem to be … The girl/boy at the front/back …
- Describe the atmosphere. Say what the people are probably feeling/thinking.
  The runners/parents/might be thinking (that) … I suppose the parents …

> **Tip**
>
> Don't **answer questions** with just *yes* or *no*.
> Say: *Yes, I do. /Yes, I am./ No, I don't./No, I'm not./ No, I don't think so*, etc.
>
> If you repeat an idea or opinion, try to express it differently.

c) *Prepare to answer questions which have to do with the picture indirectly, for example about sports or competitions. Listen to the questions on your CD (🎧 28) and prepare two sentences for each answer. Make notes first and practise your answers with them. Then speak freely without them. You can record your answers.*

13 Asking about and giving opinions

▸ SF (pp. 125–126) • WB (pp. 74–75)

a) Look at the picture and read the phrases in boxes 1 and 2 below.

1

What/Why do you think …?
Don't you think that …?
Do you agree that …?
What's your opinion about …?
Wouldn't it be better to …?
What can you …?
What advice would you give?
What should … do?

2

In my opinion, …
I (dis)agree (that) …
I really don't think …
I feel/believe (that) …
I don't think that would be a good idea …
I can't imagine …
I don't think people …
I would advise … to …
I think he should …
The problem seems to be that …

Tip

Polite phrases for the examiner/interviewer:

Could you repeat that, please?
Could you explain that again, please?
Sorry, I can't quite follow you.
Sorry, but I didn't quite understand/catch what you said.
Sorry, but what exactly do I have to do?
Does that mean that I have to …?

b) Think about four questions to ask a partner about the picture. Use the phrases in box 1 for ideas. Write notes in the space below. You can record your questions.

What do you think is happening in the picture?

c) Give your opinion on what is happening in the picture, using phrases from box 2 above. Also, give advice on what you think the boy could/should do now and in future. First, make notes below, then talk for about two minutes. You can record your opinion.

In my opinion, there will always be bullying at school if nobody … I would advise the boy to tell …

NOTES

5413
5414

14 Comparing pictures (Collecting arguments) ▸ WB (pp. 74–75)

a) Collect arguments for and against having a weekend job or learning for exams at the weekend. Choose one of the topics and make notes in the box below.

Doing a weekend job	Learning for school at the weekend
For	**For**
______________________	______________________
______________________	______________________
______________________	______________________
______________________	______________________
______________________	______________________
Against	**Against**
______________________	______________________
______________________	______________________
______________________	______________________
______________________	______________________

b) Talk about the advantages and disadvantages of the topic you have chosen and give your opinion about it. Practise giving your arguments first with your notes, then without them. You can record your talk.

15 The digital age (Talking about cartoons) ▸ SF (p. 126) • WB (pp. 74–75)

Talk about the cartoon using ideas/phrases from the box and your own ideas.

1 Describe what you see, what the people are doing.
2 What is the cartoonist's message? Is it clear enough?
3 Give your opinion on the cartoon. Do you like it?

The cartoon shows ...
We see the mother standing at ... The son is sitting at ...
The son tells the mother that ... although ...

The cartoonist wants to say/comment on ...
teenagers and communication – the digital age – too much use of electronic media – contact with family members – talk to parents less – prefer to blog ...

WRITING

16 Writing better sentences 1 (Adding adjectives and adverbs)

▸ WB (p. 75)

Look again at the picture story on p. 16 of your workbook. Complete the sentences below with words from the boxes to make the story more interesting.

Adjectives	Adverbs and adverb phrases
awful • excited • funny • brown • good-looking • interesting • old • small • sporty • blond	easily • excitedly • loudly • luckily • quickly • suddenly • one evening • the next day • in the next town • all the time • on the way

Picture 1: One evening Sophie suddenly received a text from her boyfriend, Tom. ______ she read his message, but she couldn't believe what it said – he had dumped her.

Picture 2: Sophie was shocked. She called her best friend for advice. Her friend told her to keep busy and not to sit at home thinking about him ______.

Picture 3: Sophie called her cousin and decided to visit her for the weekend.

Picture 4: ______, Sophie ______ packed her rucksack and left home on her ______ moped. The weather was just the way she felt – ______. It was raining.

Picture 5: ______ she stopped at a ______ café ______. She was thinking about Tom, so she didn't notice that a ______ young guy with ______ hair had also entered the café.

Picture 6: The young guy sat down at the next table. He was wearing a ______ jacket and jeans. He started an ______ conversation about mopeds and told a ______ story about his moped that made Sophie laugh. They chatted ______ and laughed a lot.

Picture 7: Sophie and the young guy left the café together, talking ______. ______, it had stopped raining. They would meet again the next day. And Tom? Who was Tom? Had she forgotten him already?

5616

17 Writing better sentences 2 (Using linking words) ▸ WB (p. 75)

a) Mark the correct word.

1 (When/If) Dominic and Afra get married next week, it will be a Muslim wedding[1].

2 (Because/Although) there are some disadvantages to mixed relationships, there are also many advantages.

3 Often the young couple are happy, (but/because) their parents are not.

4 Sometimes a relationship does not last (because/so that) the different religions make everyday life difficult.

Tip

Linking words improve[2] the style of your texts – and get you better marks in exams. Use them whenever possible. Check your word order after the linking word: S-V-O.

b) Choose the correct linking word from the box to complete the sentences below.

after • although • because • before • so • so ... that • when

1 ____________ young people fall in love, they do not usually care about religion.

2 Problems often start ____________ the couple have lived together for some time.

3 Sometimes the partners don't know much about each other's religion, ____________ they are not tolerant enough.

4 Mixed relationships often work well ____________ the partners respect each other's religion.

5 Sometimes one partner changes to the religion of the other, ____________ there won't be any problems.

c) Join the two sentences using the linking word in brackets.

1 Annabel and Ranjiv's relationship is successful. They have different religions. (although)

Annabel and Ranjiv's relationship is successful, although they have different religions.

2 Mixed relationships were not easily accepted[3] 50 years ago. They are not unusual[4] today. (which)

____

3 Annabel and Ranjiv have been together for two years. Ranjiv is a Hindu. (who)

____

4 There is often a problem with children. The parents cannot agree on the religion for the child. (because)

____

5 It is possible to be tolerant and understanding towards a partner with a different religion. Mixed relationships show it. (that)

____

____

5717
5718

[1]wedding ['wedɪŋ] *Hochzeit* [2]improve [ɪm'pru:v] *(sich) verbessern* [3]accept [ək'sept] *akzeptieren* [4]unusual [ʌn'ju:ʒuəl] *ungewöhnlich*

18 Collecting and organizing ideas ▸ SF (p. 141) • WB (pp. 75–76)

a) Read the ideas below. Then cross out, order and number the list, so that you can write a short article of about 120 words. Finally, rewrite the finished list in your exercise book.

Notes: **A good job interview**
- arrive early
- dress neatly
- girls: not too much make-up
- boys: not your oldest jeans and T-shirt!
- find out info about the company before the interview
- ask questions about the company
- ask about training programmes
- don't ask about money
- prepare answers to standard questions
- prepare to talk about your qualifications, skills and personal qualities
- smile when you say goodbye
- wait until you are offered a seat[1]
- be polite, friendly, interested
- thank the interviewer
- know your strengths and weaknesses
- talk about your work experience
- keep eye contact with the interviewer
- say why you would be good for the job/apprenticeship
- send a short letter of thanks on the next day
- speak clearly, not fast

Tip

When you **brainstorm ideas**, write down **all** your ideas, even if they don't seem very useful. Then go through your finished list and **cross out** the ideas that you decide not to use. **Order** and **number** the good ideas.

b) Use your list and write a short article of about 120 words for your school mag: 'How to do well at an interview'. Write in your exercise book.

Tip

Make a **check list** of your own 'favourite mistakes' and look for these mistakes when you read through your finished text. Read it more than once. Look for different kinds of mistakes each time: e.g. spelling, tenses, word order, *do/does/did*, etc., *ing*-forms or *to*-infinitives, uncountable nouns, articles.

19 Correcting mistakes ▸ WB (p. 76)

Correct this e-mail from Maria to her cousin in the UK. Mark the mistakes and correct them in the space below.

Hi Becca!
Here I am at last! Sorry I didn't write to you since Christmas. I've been at home with a very bad cold since a week. I had a temperature too, so the doctor said I must to stay in the bed, but tomorrow I go to school again. My best news are that I will do volunteer work after school, maybe in India for six months. My teacher gave me some advices, and I have got a lot of informations from the internet. Our neighbours daughter also has gone to India last year, and she did some really intresting work in a school. I would like working on an environmental project. Mum has told to me that you have done volunteer work after you left school. What did you? Maybe we can talk over it when I see you to Easter[2]. I already look forward to see you all again. I'm sure we have a great time. I hope the whether will be good. If not, we can go shoping. And I'd like to go to London again by the train, and make some photos like we did last time. OK. That's enough for today. I call you again soon, maybe next weekend.
Love to everybody, Maria

Correct

I haven't written, for a week, I had to,

5919

[1]seat [siːt] *Sitz, Platz* [2]Easter [ˈiːstə] *Ostern*

20 Structuring a written text (Written discussion 1)

► SF (p. 148) • WB (pp. 75–76)

a) Read the four text parts about: Mobile phones should be banned from school. *It is not important to understand every new word.*

☐

First, there may be cases where parents need to contact their children, for example if there is a problem at home or an important change of plan. Children can let their parents know where they are, for example if they are going to be late home. Another reason is that one can argue that a mobile phone gives both students and parents a degree of security outside the home, as the student can always be contacted.

☐

I think there are more disadvantages than advantages of allowing students to have mobiles in the classroom. Students can always be contacted in school in case of an emergency[1] at home, so they needn't have mobiles in school. In my opinion, mobiles should only be used in free time, not in school time.

☐

The mobile has become part of today's youth culture and is high up on a teen's list of 'must haves'. A mobile is a useful thing to have, but the important question is: should students be allowed to take mobiles to school?

☐

First, lessons are interrupted and concentration is easily lost. This is unfair both to the class and to the teacher.
Second, it may be possible to cheat in tests by getting outside help – there are known cases of this. Also, expensive designer phones have become status symbols and for this reason have no place in school. They may encourage trouble or bullying. Finally, another reason is that photos and videos from mobiles can be misused, for example they can be posted on the internet without permission[2].

b) Put the text parts in the correct order. Write the numbers 1–4 in the boxes.

c) Label the parts in a): Introduction | First point of view | Second point of view | Conclusion

d) Choose the correct topic sentence below for each part in a) and write it in the box above.

- However, other people think there are more reasons to ban mobiles in school.
- After looking at arguments on both sides, I think mobiles should be banned from school.
- A large percentage of school students from the age of ten or younger own a mobile phone.
- On the one hand, many parents and students will say that mobiles are necessary in school.

e) Write a list of words/phrases from the text in a) that are used to link ideas:

First, ...

[1]emergency [ɪˈmɜːdʒənsi] *Notfall* [2]permission [pəˈmɪʃn] *Erlaubnis*

21 What's your opinion? (Written discussion 2)

▸ SF (p. 148) • WB (pp. 75–76)

Tip

Remember that it is often better to begin with the point of view that you **don't support**. If you think students **shouldn't do community service**, first say why some people think community service for all teenagers would be a good idea.

a) Collect arguments for and against this statement:

Teenagers should do six months' community service after they leave school.

Make notes below in the boxes.

Arguments <u>for</u> doing community service

young people should do something for others; volunteers are always needed;

Arguments <u>against</u> doing community service

six months too long;

b) Match the phrases below to the section of the outline where you could use them (sometimes in two sections). Write a number 1–4 next to the phrase.

1 **Introduction** – state the topic and say why it is important
2 **Arguments** – first point of view
3 **Arguments** – second point of view
4 **Conclusion** – sum up the arguments and give your own point of view

Phrase	No.	Phrase	No.
In my opinion, …	4	So the question is, should … or not?	
On the one hand, …	2	For example, I know …	
People often say that …		That is why I think …	
This topic is important because …		First/Second/Finally, …	
A good example of this is …		Other people/students disagree. They think that …	
To sum up, I believe that …		Another reason is that …	
However, lots of people feel that …		After looking at both sides, …	
On the other hand, …			

c) Produce a written discussion on this topic using ideas from a) and phrases from b). Write at least 120 words in your exercise book.

22 Writing a report (Giving information: The 5 Ws + how) ▸ WB (pp. 75–76)

a) Read the following text and underline the information which answers the 5 Ws (who, why, when, what, where) and how. Then write down the information.

On 8th December 1980 at 10.50 pm the former *Beatle* John Lennon was murdered by Mark David Chapman. Lennon was shot in the back four times with a gun. The killing took place in New York City, at the entrance[1] to the exclusive apartment house, the Dakota Building, on West 72nd Street, where Lennon and Yoko Ono lived. At the time of the killing the motive was unclear, but Chapman had a history of mental[2] illness.

When: 8th December 1980 at 10.50 pm

Who:

b) Read the notes which a reporter made about an accident. Then use them to write the newspaper report. Include all the facts and decide on a suitable order in which to give the information. Do not add opinions.

Tip

Give the reader important information in the first few sentences: **who** the text is about, **what** happened or took place, **where**, **when** and **why** it happened and sometimes **how** it happened. The order is not always the same.
Topics of reports are often crimes and accidents, but also events – weddings[3], deaths, visits, holidays, special days.

NOTES

boy 13, doing paper round before school, knocked off bike, yesterday at 7.20 am, hit by silver Toyota Auris, Willow Road Merton, car driving too fast, couldn't stop, wet road, boy crossed road without looking, driver, 35, mechanic from Didcot, boy taken to St. Mary's hospital, broken leg, in shock

Accident report

A 13-year-old boy was knocked off his bike while he was doing his paper round before school. He was hit by

c) Research the following topics and answer the 5 Ws (+ how?). Write a report in your exercise book.

1 The marriage[4] of Robbie Williams

2 The death of Michael Jackson

[1]entrance ['entrəns] *Eingang* [2]mental ['mentl] *geistig* [3]wedding ['wedɪŋ] *Hochzeit* [4]marriage ['mærɪdʒ] *Ehe*

READING

23 Fitting in ▸ WB (pp. 72–73)

a) Before you read, skim the text and mark the correct answer: A, B or C.

The text …

- A gives information to parents.
- B describes a typical teenage problem.
- C is about bullying.

Tip

To get a first impression of the topic of the text, look at the **title**, **headings**, **picture(s)**, and words in **bold** type.

Who are your peers[1]?

Your peers are the people around you, people your age, for example your classmates, the people in your sports team, kids at your youth club or in the neighbourhood.

What is peer pressure[2]?

People are sometimes persuaded to do things (or not to do things) by their peers. If your peers are doing it, you may feel that you should do it too. But the things that peers persuade you to do may be good or bad.

Positive peer pressure

Good things are, for example, that you can learn positive values and healthy attitudes from your peers. They can motivate you to learn and discover your potential, to be ambitious, to join a club or do a sport, to help in the community. They can influence your opinions in a positive way.

Negative peer pressure

Your peers can also influence you negatively. Young people are often persuaded to do things that are bad for them – even if they do not want to. Typical examples are drinking alcohol, smoking at an early age, missing school without parental permission. Some things are not only bad but dangerous or illegal, such as shoplifting, stealing or taking drugs. Being the only one to say no is hard – it takes a lot of courage and strength of character.

Why do people let themselves be influenced?

People give in to peer pressure because they want to be accepted by the peer group, they want to fit in. They think that it is better to go with the crowd, to belong. Teens sometimes do bad things because they are afraid of losing 'friends', being laughed at, or being excluded from the group. Often they are 'dared' to do something wrong or illegal. They want to prove that they can take risks or they want to impress the group leader, so they do it – and end up in trouble with the law, or in hospital …

Does peer pressure go away?

Not only teenagers are influenced by peers. You always have peers and you may experience peer pressure not only at school but also later as an apprentice or in your job. But teenagers feel more pressure from their peers than adults. Maybe this is because adults have more experience of life's lessons.

What you can do

Be critical. Choose your friends carefully. Spend time with peers who have the same values and attitudes as you. One really good friend is worth more than a whole group who just want to control you. Do only what you feel is right. Do not run with the crowd if you do not want to. Do not do things you might regret. If you are worried, talk to an older teen, a brother or sister. Being strong will give you self-confidence, and remember, true friends will respect you more for standing up for yourself.

6401

[1]peers [pɪəz] *Gleichaltrige* [2]peer pressure [ˈpreʃə] *Druck/Einfluss der Clique*

b) Match the sentences to the correct endings.

1 Your peers can influence you ...	• motivate you to do positive things.
2 Peer pressure is ...	• they want to be accepted by their peers.
3 Peers who are good friends can ...	• that you have strength of character.
4 When your peers pressure you, you should ...	• in a positive or negative way.
5 If you can say no, you show ...	• a problem lots of teenagers experience.
6 Teenagers sometimes give in to peer pressure because ...	• do what you feel is right.

c) Complete the sentences using information from the text. Write in your exercise book.

1 Your peers are ...
2 Positive peer pressure means ...
3 Peer pressure is often negative. For example, when ...
4 There are a few reasons why young people run with the crowd. For example, ...
5 You have a strong character if you ...

Tip

Scan the text and look for **key words**. Then read around them to find the answer. Don't copy from the text. Try to use your own words.
Keep your sentences simple.

24 Working out the meaning of words ▸ *WB (p. 72)*

Look at the text in exercise 23 (p. 62) again. How did you work out the meaning of the words that are new? Write the words below in the lists with their German meaning. Some words fit in two lists. Decide what helped you most.

persuade • values • motivate • potential • influence • parental • permission • shoplifting • courage • accept • exclude • dare • prove • risk • critical • worth • regret • self-confidence

From the context	Like a German word	From a part of the word or from the word family
persuade – überreden	motivate – motivieren	values – Werte

25 What do UK teenagers think? ▸ *WB (pp. 72–73)*

a) *Skim the text. What does the text report? Tick A, B or C.*

A Teenagers' problems with family and society.
B Mainly negative attitudes of British teenagers.
C Mainly positive values of British teenagers.

Britain's teenagers: what do they think?

There are over 5.5 million teenagers (13–19) in Britain. Teens are not always popular. Many people think they are lazy, noisy troublemakers who do not show much respect for adults. People think teenagers want to have fun without responsibility. But this seems to be true only for a minority of teenagers. Surveys which asked teenagers about their attitudes, beliefs and lifestyle have found that their views are quite conservative. Here are some interesting findings:

Family values

- Over 90% of UK teenagers believe in marriage.
- Six out of ten teenagers think it is better to get married before having children.
- Two-thirds think that too many teenage pregnancies are terminated.
- 8,000 under 16s become pregnant every year, and 40,000 under 18s. Teenage birth rates in Britain are twice as high as in Germany and six times higher than in Holland.
- The survey *Typical Young People* (commissioned by the *Scout Association* in January 2007) found that most teenagers have respect for their parents and usually listen to what they have to say.
- 70% of teenagers say that their parents let them make their own decisions.
- Two-thirds of teenage girls see their mother as their role model[1], not a female media star.
- When boys were asked about their role models, three times more named their father as a role model, not footballers or rappers.
- Young people do not wish to have an extravagant lifestyle like many media stars.
- Most teenagers just want to earn enough money to be financially independent.

Social values

- A 2010 survey found that most British teens have democratic and tolerant views. They expect to vote in future but will not join a political party as they are not much interested in political topics.
- Teens in Britain care about their community and the environment. They are interested in what is happening, even if they are not actively involved.
- Over 80% have a strong sense of national identity and are proud to be British.

6603

[1]role model [ˈrəʊl mɒdl] *Vorbild*

b) Read the statements below. Are they true or false? Write F or T.

1 Some people think that teenagers in the UK show little respect for adults. ...... T
2 Surveys find that the statement in 1) may be true. ...... ☐
3 Fewer than 10% of British teenagers do not believe in marriage. ...... ☐
4 60% think it is better to get married before you start a family. ...... ☐
5 Holland has the highest rate of single teenage mothers. ...... ☐
6 Over 60% of teens think their mother has a positive influence[1] on them. ...... ☐
7 Teenagers think media stars make good role models. ...... ☐
8 Seven out of ten teenagers say their parents let them decide things themselves. ...... ☐
9 More than 20% of UK teenagers are not proud to be British. ...... ☐
10 Teenagers in general take an interest in environmental and community issues[2]. ...... ☐

Tip

Look for **key words** in the questions and mark them before you read.
There are different ways of expressing numbers.
For example:
- *70% = 7 out of 10*
- *66% = two-thirds*
- *75% = three-quarters*
- *over = more than*
- *under = less/fewer than.*

c) Find and write statements from the text which mean the same as the following:

1 Teenagers are often seen in a negative light.

Teens are not always popular. (l. 2)

2 Less than ten percent of UK teens think that getting married is not important.

______

______

3 More than sixty percent of female teens say their mum is the person they look up to most.

______

______

4 British teenagers take an interest in community and environmental issues, even if they do not always play an active role.

______

______

Tip

Look for **words** in the sentences and text that mean **the same**.
For example:
negative – bad
media – press
mum – mother.

[1]influence [ˈɪnfluəns] *Einfluss* [2]issue [ˈɪʃuː] *Thema, Problem*

MEDIATION

26 Slam – a book to make you laugh (From English into German) ▸ WB (p. 77)

You have read the book Slam by Nick Hornby in English. Now you want to recommend it to your friends. Tell them in German what the book is about. You can make notes in your exercise book first.

Tip

Leave out details and names that are not important for the main events of the storyline. Don't translate.

16-year-old Sam lives in London with his young, divorced mother Annie. There isn't much money, so Sam doesn't expect much from life. But he is happy because he lives for skating. He has a poster in his room of his big hero, the skater Tony Hawk. Sam talks to him as a friend, as if he was there in his room.
Sam also has a new girlfriend, Alicia, but after a time Sam wants to dump her. Then – slam! Alicia gets pregnant. Sam is scared, so he runs away to the coast. He thinks he can solve the problem if he throws his mobile phone into the sea. But he can't find work, so he returns home. Alicia's parents, who are university teachers, want her to get rid of Sam – and the baby. They say Sam has ruined her life. Sam's mother also thinks that his life is now ruined. Sam often has dreams which show him his future – and that he doesn't know how to care for a baby. He moves into Alicia's house, but he is not welcome there, so he moves back to his mother's flat. He breaks off his relationship with Alicia because both know that it won't work. Later Sam has a new girlfriend called Alex, and Alicia a new boyfriend called Carl. So what will happen in the end?

27 A holiday in the Canadian Rockies (From English into German) ▸ WB (p. 77)

Tell your parents in German why a trip to the Rockies would make a great holiday for you and your teen sister/brother.

Tip

Report **facts**, not opinions.
Decide which facts are important. For example, in this text **what you can do** is more important than place names.

FUN FOR TEENS IN THE ROCKIES

Teens will never get bored on a family vacation in the Canadian Rockies. There's so much to see and do. Here are some suggestions for great entertainment and fun activities.

Teens love action, so why not go hiking up Sentinel Pass, above beautiful Moraine Lake. It's the highest hiking trail in Canada! Or how about a hike up Sulphur Mountain – that's quite a challenge[1] too!

Teens love water sports. Our lakes are awesome – even if the water is freezing cold. Try a swim before breakfast! But that's not all. On the Kicking Horse River you'll find the coolest whitewater rafting, and in Kicking Horse Mountain Resort the most exciting mountain bike trails! While you're there, check out the grizzly bears, and the wolves at the Wolf Centre in Golden. Go canoeing or fishing for rainbow trout[2]! Warm up with a swim in the hot springs in Miette!

Teens love climbing. Learn all about rock climbing on a real mountain face with a qualified mountain guide! More cool pictures of a lifetime.

Teens love adventure. Take a trip on horseback into the backcountry. Stay overnight at a backcountry lodge[3] in the mountain wilderness! Just you and nature.

[1]challenge [ˈtʃæləndʒ] *Herausforderung* [2]trout [traʊt] *Forelle* [3]lodge [lɒdʒ] *Hütte*

28 Learning English in England (From English into German) ▸ WB (p. 77)

You would like to do a language course in London in the summer holidays. You find this information online. Write notes in German so that you can give your parents details about where the school is, the courses, accommodation[1] and prices.

The Prince School of English

We are a private language school with 40 years' experience of teaching English to foreign students. Our school is located near Regent's Park, in a quiet residential part of London, within easy reach of the sights. Why choose us? We offer:

- a **wide range[2] of courses** for all levels and age groups.
- highly **qualified**, friendly teachers.
- **small groups** of 8–10 students.
- exam preparation for **all main exams**.
- **special-emphasis courses**, e.g. in pronunciation/speaking.
- courses in business, IT, and British history and culture.
- modern classrooms with electronic media.
- coffee bar serving snacks, soft drinks and light lunches.
- computer lounge with free broadband internet.
- an organised **leisure and activities programme** including day trips, a musical and museums.
- **individual consultation[3]** on the right course for you.
- help with **accommodation** of your choice.

Please call us for detailed course information and prices.
00443277987610

29 A visit to the Bavaria film studios (From German to English) ▸ WB (p. 77)

You are in Munich with your cousin from England. You would like to show her the Bavaria film studios. Your cousin asks some questions. Use your notes from the website below and answer her questions in English.

- What is there to see and do?
- Will I understand what's happening?
- When's the best time to go there?
- Is it expensive?
- Is there anywhere to eat?
- How do we get there?
- Can we take photos?
- Can we take the dog?

Tip

If you don't know important words, **paraphrase** or say the sentence differently with words that you know. For example:
Führung – a tour with a guide
ermäßigt – cheaper for students
ausweisen – show proof of your age

BAVARIA FILMSTADT

Führungen:

- finden im Sommer jede Stunde statt – auch sonntags, letzte Führung um 16.00 Uhr, dauert ca. 90 Minuten, gibt es auch um 13.00 Uhr täglich auf Englisch
- ermäßigter Preis für Schüler €10 (an der Kasse mit Foto ausweisen)
- Kinofilmkulissen[4], z.B. „Das Boot", TV-Serien: „Marienhof", „Sturm der Liebe"

- Attraktionen gibt es auch im Freien – Laufschuhe und Regenkleidung
- Stunt Show – Zeiten in Erfahrung bringen! Hund darf mit! Fotografieren und Video erlaubt, Fast-food-Restaurant offen 9.30–18.00 Uhr, Souvenir-Shop und Snackpoint
- Anfahrt: Straßenbahn 25 Richtung Grünwald > Haltestelle Bavariafilmplatz, dann ca. 10 Minuten zu Fuß

6304

[1]accommodation [əˌkɒməˈdeɪʃn] *Unterkunft* [2]range [reɪndʒ] *Reihe, Auswahl* [3]consultation [ˌkɒnslˈteɪʃn] *Beratung* [4]film set *Filmkulisse*

LANGUAGE

30 A postcard from San Francisco (Simple present or present progressive) ▸ WB (p. 77)

*Complete Marie's postcard with the correct form of the verb: **simple present** or **present progressive**.*

Tip

Use the **simple present** with *often, usually, never, always, every day* and verbs such as *like, love, know, believe, seem, look, see.*
Use the **present progressive** with *now, at the moment, today.*

Hi Sarah!
Just imagine! We *'re spending* (spend) a week in San Francisco! You'll be surprised because we ______ (usually, not go) on holiday at Easter. But Dad's American friend ______ (live) here, so we ______ (visit) the family now. We ______ (love) it here. ♥Steve ______ (not like) writing postcards, so at the moment he ______ (take) photos. Every day we *see* (see) something different.
We ______ (often, not get) lost. If we ______ (look) like lost tourists, someone always ______ (help) us.
We ______ (have) a really great time – and we ______ (not miss) dirty old Liverpool! Will be home next week. ☹
Love, Marie

6801

31 A questionnaire (Question forms) ▸ GF 2 (p. 153)

Write the following questions in English for a questionnaire on free-time activities.

QUESTIONNAIRE ON FREE-TIME ACTIVITIES

1 Benutzt du den Computer jeden Tag? *Do you use the computer every day?*
2 Wie viele Stunden verbringst du täglich am Computer? *How many hours do you spend on the computer every day?*
3 Besitzt du ein Handy? ______
4 Wie viele Gespräche führst du im Schnitt jeden Tag? ______
5 Welche Sportarten magst du am liebsten? ______
6 Was für Musik hörst du gern? ______
7 Liest du gern Zeitschriften? ______
8 Wie viele Zeitschriften kaufst du? ______
9 Bist du mal auf einem Rock-Konzert gewesen? ______
10 Bist du letztes Jahr in Urlaub gefahren? ______
11 Wo bist du hingefahren? ______
12 Bist du mal mit Freunden in Urlaub gefahren? ______

6802
6803

32 A true romance (Simple past or past progressive)

▸ WB (p. 78)

*Complete the text with the correct verb form: **simple past** or **past progressive**.*

The couple ___met___ (meet) in September 2001 when they ___were studying___ (study) art history in their first year at St Andrew's University in Scotland. HE first really ______ (notice) how attractive SHE was when SHE ______ (model) clothes at a university fashion show. In their second year, they ______ (get) to know each other well when they ______ (share) a house with friends. They ______ (not talk) openly about their relationship. The press ______ (not find out) about it for sure until 2004, while the couple ______ (spend) a skiing holiday in Switzerland. Paparazzi ______ (take) photos of HER with HIM and HIS father when they ______ (wait) at a ski lift. In 2007 they ______ (break up) but got back together again some months later. While HE ______ (do) military service in the RAF[1], SHE ______ (not work). HIS grandmother ______ (not like) that, so SHE quickly ______ (look) for a job. The couple finally ______ (get married) on 29th April 2011 – and now SHE doesn't need a job. Who are they?

6903

Tip

Use the **simple past** to report **when** something happened in the past.
Use the **past progressive** to say what **was happening** at a time in the past, often with *while, just when, as*.

33 WORDS Describing people

***a)** Complete the sentences with a suitable adjective from the box.*

arrogant • easy-going • good-looking • honest • jealous • reliable • romantic • shy • unfriendly

1 Vicky's new boyfriend is very ______ but he knows it so he's pretty ______.

2 Sandra's boyfriend doesn't like her to talk to other boys. He soon gets ______.

3 The new girl is ______. She's already telling everybody what to do.

4 Tom isn't very ______. He's often late for work and he forgets things.

5 I'm sure that what my boyfriend says is true. He's always ______.

6 Don't be ______ at the interview. Smile and be confident.

7 I like friends who are relaxed and ______, not too serious.

8 Charlotte's boyfriend isn't very ______. He always takes her to football matches and horror films.

***b)** Write more adjectives (positive and negative) to describe people.*

☺ friendly, ______

______

6904

☹ lazy, ______

[1]RAF = Royal Air Force

34 WORDS Hobbies and free-time activities

a) *Choose words from the box that go with the verbs below. Sometimes there is more than one.*

cartoons • cards • computer games • cycling • DVDs • e-mails • judo • karate • magazines • models • music • out • photos • riding • shopping • sport • swimming • the guitar • the internet

do *judo, karate, sport*

draw

go

hang

listen to

make

play

read

surf

take

watch

write

b) *Write four sentences about what you do and when you usually do it.*

I usually listen to music before I go to bed.

7005

35 Explaining words (Paraphrasing)

▸ *WB (p. 75)*

If you don't know the English word for what you want to say, you can paraphrase it. Paraphrasing is useful in mediation. Choose some of these phrases to paraphrase the words below:

It's like ... It's the same as/similar to ... It's someone who ...
It's something that ... It's a place where ...
It's a (general word) that ... It's something you use/need to ...

Tip

Use **simple words** that you know, with details to make the meaning clear.

1 Azubi: *It's a young person who works in a company or factory to train for a job.*

2 Mittlere Reife: *It's an important exam*

3 Werkstatt:

4 Praktikum:

5 Kunde/-in:

36 WORDS Word families

Complete the chart. Then complete the sentences below with the correct words in the correct form.

VERB	NOUN	ADJECTIVE
advise	*advice, adviser*	–
________	application	–
________	argument	–
choose	________	–
decide	________	–
________	explanation	–
–	office	________
organize	________	________
________	success	________
–	________	strong

I've ________ for a job. Can you give me any ________ for my interview tomorrow? – At an interview they often ask you about your ________ and weaknesses. Even if you don't agree with the interviewer, don't ________ with him or her! Good luck! I hope you' ll be ________.

7107

37 WORDS Opposites

Find and write pairs of opposites below. Then write four sentences with pairs of opposites in your exercise book.

boring • fat • hard-working • lend • majority • relaxed • soft • thin • well	badly • borrow • *exciting* • hard • lazy • minority • nervous • skinny • thick

boring – exciting

________ ________ ________

7108

38 Dating (Prepositions)

Underline the correct preposition.

1 Kelly has dumped her boyfriend. She said they were too different (of/from) each other.
2 She said he never stopped talking (about/of) football and she was fed up (of/with) it.
3 (After/In) my opinion, she did the right thing. You can't stay (by/with) a person like that.
4 Could you ever fall in love (with/in) a person much older than you?
5 I would never date anyone I met (in/on) the internet, because I wouldn't know enough (about/over) them.
7109 6 My 17-year-old sister is a single mum, but she gets a lot of help (of/from) her boyfriend.

SF LISTENING AND READING SKILLS

SF Listening ▶ *p. 132*

Was muss ich beim *Listening* beachten?

Vor dem Hören:

- Überlege, worum es in dem Hörtext gehen wird. Frag dich, was du schon über das Thema weißt.
- Lies die Aufgaben gut durch, damit du weißt, worauf du achten sollst:
  - auf die **Hauptgedanken** oder die **Kernaussage** des Textes, z. B. wenn du sagen sollst, um welches Thema es geht, oder welche Meinung der Sprecher zu dem Thema hat.
  - auf bestimmte **Details**, z. B. wenn du Namen, Uhrzeiten, Jahreszahlen heraushören sollst.
- Bereite dich darauf vor, Notizen zu machen. Leg z. B. eine Tabelle oder Liste an.

Beim Hören:

- Keine Panik! Du musst nicht alles verstehen. Konzentriere dich auf das Wesentliche. Oft werden wichtige Informationen auch wiederholt.
- Achte auf Geräusche und unterschiedliche Stimmen. Was ein Sprecher/eine Sprecherin besonders betont, das ist wichtig!
- Wenn du gezielt nach Informationen suchst, denk an die Aufgabe und lass dich von anderen Einzelheiten nicht ablenken. Aufgepasst: die Informationen, die du suchst, kommen vielleicht in einer anderen Reihenfolge vor, als du sie erwartest.
- Manche Signalwörter machen es dir leichter, den Hörtext zu verstehen:
  - Aufzählung: **and**, **another**, **too**
  - Gegensatz: **although**, **but**
  - Grund, Folge: **because**, **so**, **so that**
  - Vergleich: **larger/older/... than**, **more**, **most**
  - Reihenfolge: **before**, **after**, **then**, **next**, **later**, **when**, **at last**, **at the same time**
- Mache kurze Notizen, z. B. Anfangsbuchstaben, Symbole oder Stichworte.

Nach dem Hören:

- Vervollständige deine Notizen sofort.
- Konzentriere dich beim zweiten Hören auf das, was du beim ersten Mal nicht gut verstanden hast.

READING COURSE

Working out the meaning of words ▶ *p. 134*

Was hilft dir, unbekannte Wörter zu verstehen?

1. **Bilder** zeigen oft die Dinge, die du im Text nicht verstehst. Wenn es Bilder zum Text gibt, dann schau sie dir vor dem Lesen genau an.
2. Oft hilft dir der **Textzusammenhang**, z. B. *When we* ***reached*** *the station, Judy went to the ticket machine to buy our tickets.*
3. Manche englischen Wörter werden **ähnlich wie im Deutschen** geschrieben oder ausgesprochen, z. B. **excellent**, **millionaire**, **nation**, **reality**.
4. Manchmal stecken in unbekannten Wörtern **bekannte Teile**, z. B. **friendliness**, **helpless**, **understandable**, **gardener**, **tea bag**, **waiting room**.

Skimming and scanning ▶ *p. 134*

Skimming: Lesen, um sich einen Überblick zu verschaffen

Beim **Skimming** überfliegst du einen Text schnell, um dir einen ersten **Überblick** zu verschaffen, worum es geht. Du willst herausfinden, ob ein Text, den du im Internet oder in einem Buch gefunden hast, überhaupt nützliche Informationen zu deinem Thema (z. B. für ein Referat) enthält. Achte beim Skimming auf:

- die **Überschrift**
- die **Zwischenüberschriften** und **hervorgehobene** Wörter oder Sätze
- die **Bilder** und **Bildunterschriften**
- den **ersten** und **letzten Satz** jedes Absatzes
- **Grafiken**, **Statistiken** und die **Quelle** des Textes.

Scanning: Lesen, um nach bestimmten Informationen zu suchen

Beim **Scanning** suchst du in einem Text nach **bestimmten Informationen**, die z.B. für ein Referat wichtig sind. Dazu brauchst du nicht den gesamten Text zu lesen, sondern du suchst nach Schlüsselwörtern (**key words**) und liest nur dort genauer, wo du sie findest. Geh dabei so vor:

Schritt 1: Denk an das Schlüsselwort, nach dem du suchst, oder schreib es auf.

Schritt 2: Geh mit den Augen und dem Finger schnell durch den Text, in breiten Schlingen wie bei einem „S" oder „Z" oder von oben nach unten wie bei einem „U". Dabei hast du das Schriftbild oder das Bild des Wortes, nach dem du suchst, vor Augen. Das gesuchte Wort wird dir sofort „ins Auge springen". Lies nur dort weiter, um Näheres zu erfahren.

Schritt 3: Wenn das Schlüsselwort, nach dem du suchst, im Text nicht vorkommt, überleg dir, welche anderen Wörter mit den benötigten Informationen zu tun haben, und such nach diesen.

Finding the main ideas of a text ▸ *p. 135*

Wie finde ich die Hauptaussagen eines Textes?

① Jeder Text dreht sich um ein Thema oder hat eine Hauptaussage. Diese findest du oft im ersten Absatz. Lies ihn deshalb besonders gründlich durch.

② Die Hauptaussage wird in der Regel durch weitere Aussagen bzw. Gedanken unterstützt. Du findest sie oft im ersten oder letzten Satz der nachfolgenden Absätze.

③ Diese weiteren Aussagen bzw. Gedanken werden meist durch Beispiele und Begründungen ergänzt.

We are people too!

By Oliver Munslow (16) – 23 August 2010

① To everybody out there that thinks young people are different, you're right! We're younger than adults. But that doesn't mean you don't need to listen to us or you don't have to respect us. We have feelings and (this might surprise some of you) we are people too.

Did you know that here in Britain every citizen under 18 has important rights? For example, we all have the right to be listened to and taken seriously, and we have the right to get together with our friends in public (as long as we respect the rights of other people and do not break the law).

② But British children aren't taken seriously until they're 18. Too many adults think that our views just don't count and that we don't deserve equal rights. Here are some examples of discrimination against teenagers from my everyday life (in fact, most of these things happened to me this week).

③ Every day I see signs on shop doors that say '2 children at a time', or 'no school bags', or even 'no children unless they are with an adult'. (...)

Tipp

Die folgenden Wörter oder Wendungen werden oft im Zusammenhang mit Begründungen oder Beispielen verwendet:
and so • **because** • **e.g. / for example** • **etc.** • **for lots of reasons** • **this shows that** • **that's why** • **...**

Drawing conclusions ▸ *p. 135*

Wie funktioniert schlussfolgerndes Lesen?

1. Die einfachste Form des schlussfolgernden Lesens besteht darin, die Informationen aus verschiedenen Textstellen zusammenzuführen. Bei dem Text *The Carbon Diaries* 2015 (Schülerbuch, S. 34–35) sollst du sagen, wie Laura, Kim und ihre Mutter zu *carbon rationing* stehen. Dazu musst du dir mehrere Stellen ansehen.

2. Manchmal steht die Antwort auf eine Frage nicht direkt im Text. Dann musst du sie dir erschließen. Du fragst dich z.B., ob Laura Brown und ihre Familie durch die Ausnahmesituation mehr gemeinsam unternehmen. Dafür musst du Aussagen im Text finden, die etwas mit der Frage zu tun haben:

   Lines 84–89: *Dad spends all night on his laptop, Mum is always lost on a bus somewhere and Kim just lives in her room – an evil ball of silence. (...)*

   Conclusion: *The family don't spend more time together because of carbon rationing. In fact, they spend less time together.*

SPEAKING AND WRITING SKILLS

SPEAKING COURSE

Having a conversation ▸ *p. 139*

Ein Gespräch beginnen

Es gibt immer mehrere Möglichkeiten:
- **wenn du etwas erfragen willst** (*z.B. den Weg oder die Uhrzeit*)
  Excuse me, do you know ... • Excuse me, can you tell me ...
- **wenn du jemanden begrüßen möchtest oder kennenlernst**
  Hi. • Hello. • Good morning/evening.
  Oft kann man das Gespräch dann mit einer allgemeinen Bemerkung weiterführen:
  Great day today! • That's a great ...
- **wenn du jemanden wiedertriffst**
  Hi, how are you doing? • Hi, ..., how are things? • Hi, ... Good to see/meet you.

Tipp

Oft hört man zur Begrüßung auch **How are you?** Es wird nicht erwartet, dass du darauf eine ausführliche Antwort gibst. Am besten sagst du einfach **Fine, thanks. How about you?**

Ein Gespräch führen

Für den weiteren Verlauf des Gesprächs sind diese Wendungen nützlich:
- **sich vorstellen:** By the way, my name's ... • I'm ... • Nice to meet you.
- **Smalltalk machen:** Have you ... before? • Have you ever ...? • Where are you from? • Do you like ...? • What about you?
- **um Hilfe bitten und anderen helfen:** Do you know where ...? • Can you tell me ...? • Sure, no problem • Why don't you ...?
- **sich verabschieden:** See you tomorrow/next week. • Bye!

Und wenn du etwas nicht verstanden hast, kannst du immer nachfragen:
Sorry, I didn't get that. • Sorry, could you say that again, please?

Taking part in a job interview ▸ *p. 139*

Sich vorbereiten

Auf ein Vorstellungsgespräch musst du dich unbedingt vorbereiten. Du solltest Fragen zu den folgenden Bereichen beantworten können:
- deine Eigenschaften (**personal qualities**), Stärken (**strengths**) und Schwächen (**weaknesses**)
- deine Interessen (**interests**) und Arbeitserfahrungen (**work experience**)
- was dich an dem Jobangebot reizt (**why you're interested in the job**).

Überleg dir auch eigene Fragen, z.B. zu deinem Tätigkeitsbereich (**What kind of work would I have to do?**) oder Tätigkeitsbeginn (**When would I have to start?**).

Im Vorstellungsgespräch

Im Vorstellungsgespräch ist es wichtig, dass du freundlich bist und dich als positiver und interessierter Mensch präsentierst.
- **bei der Begrüßung:** Hello, nice to meet you. • Good morning.
- **warum du dich bewirbst:** I'm really interested in ... • I'm good at ..., so I think ...
- **wenn es um deine Joberfahrungen geht:** I really enjoyed working with ...
- **bei der Verabschiedung:** Goodbye and thank you very much.

Tipp

- Hör gut zu, wenn du etwas gefragt wirst.
- Sprich nicht zu viel, aber auch nicht zu wenig.
- Sprich nicht zu schnell.

Having a discussion ▸ *p. 140*

Seine Meinung zum Ausdruck bringen und erklären

1. **Expressing an opinion:** In einer Diskussion ist es gut, wenn du möglichst klar und deutlich sagst, was du zu einer bestimmten Frage denkst:
   I think ... • In my opinion, ...

2. **Giving reasons and examples:** Genauso wichtig ist es, dass du Beispiele und Argumente nennst, die deine Meinung unterstützen – schließlich willst du deine Gesprächspartner von deinem Standpunkt überzeugen!
   because ... • First ... / Second ... / And finally... • For example ... • Let me explain ... • That's why ...

Auf andere in einer Diskussion reagieren

1. **Asking for clarification:** Manchmal ist es notwendig nachzuhaken, weil man ein Argument nicht verstanden hat:
   Could you say that again? • Sorry, but I don't understand what you mean.

2. **Agreeing with someone:** Wenn du die Meinung eines anderen unterstützen willst, kannst du das so zum Ausdruck bringen:
   I agree (with you/...) • That's a good point. • You're right.

3. **Disagreeing with someone:** Oft widerspricht man nicht direkt, sondern leitet seine Reaktion mit Sorry, ... oder I don't think ... ein. Zeig immer Respekt für die Meinung des oder der anderen.
   I don't think you can say ... • I see what you mean, but ... • Sorry, but that's not right. • Sorry, I don't agree with you. • Yes, but ...

SF Paraphrasing ► *p. 141*

Wie gehe ich beim *Paraphrasing* vor?

- Man kann mit einem Wort umschreiben, das dieselbe Bedeutung hat:
  to train is the same as to practise
  Oder man sagt das Gegenteil: alive is the opposite of dead
- Manchmal braucht man mehrere Wörter, z. B. wenn man etwas beschreibt oder erklärt. Dabei benutzt man ein allgemeines Wort (**general word**) und nennt weitere Eigenschaften.
  A racing car is a very fast car.
- Oder du umschreibst das Wort mit **... is/are like ...**
  A chef is like a cook, he or she is the main cook in a restaurant.
- Du kannst auch einen Relativsatz (**relative clause**) verwenden:
  A garage is a place where cars are checked and repaired.
  A nurse is a person who looks after people who are ill, usually in a hospital.
  ► *Mediation (WB, p. 77)*

WRITING COURSE

The steps of writing

1. Brainstorming – Ideen sammeln, dann sortieren (► *SF Brainstorming, p. 141*).
2. Schreiben. Dabei achte darauf,
   - deine Sätze zu verbinden und auszubauen (*Writing better sentences*)
   - deinen Text gut zu strukturieren (*Using paragraphs*)
   - bei einem Bericht die 5 Ws abzudecken (*Writing a report*).
3. Deinen Text inhaltlich und sprachlich überprüfen (*Correcting your text*)

Writing better sentences ► *p. 143*

Linking words

Eine Geschichte klingt interessanter, wenn du die Sätze mit **linking words** miteinander verbindest. Dabei gibt es mehrere Möglichkeiten:
- **Time phrases** wie at 7 o'clock, every morning, a few minutes later, then, next
- **Konjunktionen** wie although, because, but, so ... that, that, when, while
- **Relativpronomen** wie that und who

Adjektive und Adverbien

- Mit Adjektiven kannst du Personen, Orte oder Erlebnisse genauer und interessanter beschreiben.
  Vergleiche: The man looked into the room.
  ► The young man looked into the empty room.
- Mit Adverbien kannst du beschreiben, **wie** jemand etwas macht:
  The young man looked nervously into the empty room.

Using paragraphs ▶ *p. 143*

Structuring a text

Bei guten Texten lassen sich drei Hauptabschnitte erkennen:
- eine **Einleitung**, die in das Thema einführt
- ein **Hauptteil**, der meist aus mehreren Absätzen besteht
- ein **Schluss**, der den Text mit einer Zusammenfassung oder etwas Persönlichem zu einem interessanten Ende bringt.

Topic sentences

Am Anfang eines Absatzes sind kurze, einleitende Sätze (**topic sentences**) gut, weil sie den Lesern sofort sagen, worum es geht, z. B.

1. Orte: **My trip to ... was fantastic.** • **... is famous for ...** • **... is a great place.**
2. Personen: **... is great/funny/interesting/clever ...**
3. Aktivitäten: **... is great fun.** • **Lots of people ... every day.**

Wie kann ich meine Absätze interessant gestalten?

- Beginne mit einem interessanten Einstiegssatz:
  You'll never guess what happened to me today! • **Did I tell you that ...?**
- Fange für jeden neuen Aspekt einen neuen Absatz an.
- Beende deinen Text mit einer Zusammenfassung oder etwas Persönlichem.

Writing a report – structuring information ▶ *p. 144*

Worauf kommt es bei einem Bericht an?

- Gib dem Leser **eine schnelle Orientierung**, was passiert ist.
- Beginne mit **wichtigen Informationen** und gib erst dann Detailinformationen.
- Ein Bericht gibt immer Antworten auf die **5 Ws**:
  Who? What? When? Where? Why? und manchmal auch auf **How?**
- Verwende das **simple past**.

Correcting your text ▶ *p. 144*

Spelling mistakes

Lies deinen Text langsam, Wort für Wort, Buchstabe für Buchstabe. Wenn du unsicher bist, hilft dir ein Wörterbuch. Beachte folgende Regeln:

Tipp

- Manche Wörter haben Buchstaben, die man nicht spricht, aber schreibt, z. B. **knife**, **climb**.
- Manchmal ändert sich die Schreibweise, wenn ein Wort eine Endung erhält,
  z. B. **take** → **taking**, **terrible** → **terribly**, **lucky** → **luckily**,
  try → **tries** (**aber** **stay** → **stays**), **run** → **running**, **drop** → **dropped**.
- Beim Plural tritt manchmal noch ein **-e** zum **-s**, z. B. **church** → **churches**.

Grammar mistakes

Diese Tipps helfen dir, typische Fehler zu vermeiden:

Tipp

- Im **simple present** wird in der 3. Person Singular **-s** angehängt: **she knows**.
- **Unregelmäßige Verben:** Manche Verben bilden die Formen des *simple past* und des Partizip Perfekt (*past participle*) unregelmäßig. Die unregelmäßigen Formen musst du lernen. Die Liste steht auf S. 224–225.
  go – went – gone; buy – bought – bought
- **Verneinung bei Vollverben:** Im *simple present* mit ***don't/doesn't***, im *simple past* mit ***didn't***, z. B. **He doesn't speak French, he didn't learn it at school.**
- **Satzstellung**: Im Englischen gilt immer (auch im Nebensatz):
  a) subject – verb – object (S-V-O) **... when I saw my brother.**
  ... als ich meinen Bruder sah.
  b) Orts- vor Zeitangabe **I bought a nice book in town yesterday.**
  Ich habe gestern in der Stadt ein schönes Buch gekauft.

MEDIATION SKILLS

SF Mediation ► *p. 149*

Worauf muss ich bei *mediation* achten?

- Übersetze nicht alles wörtlich.
- Gib nur das Wesentliche weiter. Oft gibt dir die Fragestellung Hinweise, worauf es ankommt.
- Verwende kurze und einfache Sätze.
- Wenn du ein Wort nicht kennst, umschreibe es oder ersetze es durch ein anderes Wort.

Was kann ich tun, wenn ich ein wichtiges Wort nicht kenne?

Vielleicht findest du es manchmal schwer, mündliche Aussagen oder schriftliche Textvorlagen in die andere Sprache zu übertragen, z. B. weil:

- dein Wortschatz nicht ausreicht
- dir bekannte Wörter „im Stress" nicht einfallen
- spezielle Fachbegriffe auftauchen.

Manche Wörter kannst du umschreiben, z. B. mithilfe von Relativsätzen wie:
It's somebody/a person who ... • It's something that you use to ... • It's an animal that ... • It's a place where ...

► *Paraphrasing (WB, p. 75)*

GF 3 Talking about the present ► *p. 154*

3.1 The simple present

Dave Wilson **usually** gets the bus to school.
On Mondays his mother takes him in the car.
He **never** cycles to school because it's too far.

Das ***simple present*** wird verwendet,

◄ um über Handlungen und Ereignisse zu sprechen, die **wiederholt, regelmäßig, immer** oder **nie** geschehen (oft mit Zeitangaben wie *always, never, usually, sometimes, often, every week, on Mondays* usw.).

Dave and his family live in Manchester.
He plays hockey and collects models of old cars.

◄ um über **Dauerzustände**, **Hobbys** und **Berufe** zu sprechen.

! *He, she, it* – das „s" muss mit.

Verneinte Sätze	I don't cycle to school.	Dave doesn't walk to school.
Fragen	Do you go to school by bus? **Where** do the Wilsons live?	Does your mother take you in the car? **When** does Dave's mother take him in the car?

3.2 The present progressive

What's Dave doing? –
Just now he's cleaning his bike.

Dave (on the phone) I can't talk right now, Jack. I'm cleaning my bike.

Das ***present progressive*** wird verwendet,

◄ um über Handlungen und Ereignisse zu sprechen, die **jetzt gerade im Gange** sind (oft mit Angaben wie *at the moment, now, just*).

! Die Handlung, um die es geht, kann für einen Augenblick unterbrochen sein, z. B. durch ein Telefonat. Wichtig ist, dass sie noch nicht abgeschlossen ist.

This week Dave's grandma is staying at the Wilsons' because Dave's mum is ill.

◄ um über **vorübergehende Zustände** zu sprechen (begrenzter Zeitraum: *this week*).

Verneinte Sätze	The Wilsons aren't working.	Dave isn't watching TV.
Fragen	Are you watching TV? **What** are you doing?	Is Dave cleaning his bike? **Who** is Dave talking to?

GF 4 Talking about the past ► *pp. 155–156*

4.1 The simple past

Last Friday Katie's family flew to Spain.
Letzten Freitag ist Katies Familie nach Spanien geflogen / flog Katies Familie nach Spanien.
Two years ago the Websters moved to Bath.
Vor zwei Jahren sind die Websters nach Bath gezogen.

Wenn man über Vergangenes berichtet, benutzt man überwiegend das ***simple past***. Man beschreibt damit Handlungen, Ereignisse und Zustände, die zu einer bestimmten Zeit in der Vergangenheit *(yesterday, last Friday, two years ago, in 2003, between 2005 and 2008, ...)* stattfanden.

! Im Deutschen wird in diesen Fällen oft das Perfekt verwendet, im Englischen jedoch nicht.

Verneinte Sätze	They didn't fly to France.	Katie didn't want to go at first.
Fragen	Did you go on holiday last year? **Where** did you go?	Did Katie like it? **When** did the Websters move to Bath?

4.2 The past progressive

What were you doing yesterday at 3.30? –
I was waiting for my sister at the school doors. She was still talking to our Maths teacher.

Angela was just crossing the road when she saw her boyfriend.
Angela war gerade dabei, die Straße zu überqueren, ...

Das ***past progressive*** wird verwendet,

- um über Handlungen und Ereignisse zu sprechen, die zu einer bestimmten Zeit in der Vergangenheit noch im Gange, also noch nicht abgeschlossen waren.
- wenn man beschreiben will, was gerade vor sich ging *(she was just crossing the road)*, als etwas anderes passierte *(she saw her boyfriend)*.

Verneinte Sätze	You weren't listening.	It wasn't snowing when we left the house.
Fragen	Were you watching TV? **What** were they doing?	Was she crossing the road when it happened? **What** was she doing?

4.3 The past perfect

When Emma arrived home, her parents had already eaten.
Als Emma zu Hause eintraf, hatten ihre Eltern bereits gegessen.

Wenn man sagen will, dass etwas noch vor etwas anderem in der Vergangenheit stattgefunden hatte, dann benutzt man das ***past perfect***.

Verneinte Sätze	They hadn't gone to bed.	Emma hadn't eaten anything all day.
Fragen	Had you seen that film before? **What** had they done?	Had Emma eaten when she came home? **Where** had she been all day?

4.4 The present perfect

! Das ***present perfect*** hat mit der **Vergangenheit und mit der Gegenwart** zu tun. Es wird verwendet,

Will Smith is great. I've seen most of his films.
Luke has **already** done his Maths homework,
but he has**n't** started his French **yet**.
Have you **ever** been to Paris?
– No, I haven't. But I've **always** wanted to go.

- wenn man sagen will, **dass** jemand etwas getan hat oder **dass** etwas geschehen ist. Dabei ist nicht wichtig, wann es geschehen ist – ein genauer Zeitpunkt wird nicht genannt. Das *present perfect* steht oft mit Adverbien der unbestimmten Zeit wie *already, just, never, ever, not ... yet.*

Mel has lost her mobile. Her dad is very angry.

Oft hat die Handlung Auswirkungen auf die Gegenwart (Mels Vater ist wütend, weil sie ihr Handy verloren hat).

We've had our new car **since April**. Wir haben unser neues Auto seit April.	We've had our new car **for three months**. Wir haben unser neues Auto seit drei Monaten.
***since* + Zeitpunkt**	***for* + Zeitraum**

- für **Zustände**, die in der Vergangenheit begonnen haben und jetzt noch andauern (oft mit ***since*** bzw. ***for***).

! Im Deutschen steht in diesen Fällen meist das Präsens, im Englischen muss das *present perfect* stehen.

Verneinte Sätze	I haven't been to Paris yet.	Luke hasn't done his French homework.
Fragen	Have you been to Paris? What have you done?	Has Mel found her mobile yet? Which of these films have you seen already?

GF 5 Talking about the future ► *p. 157*

5.1 The *going to*-future

My boyfriend says he's going to be an engineer.
Mein Freund sagt, er will Ingenieur werden.

Look at those clouds. There's going to be a storm.
... Es wird ein Gewitter geben.

Das **Futur mit *going to*** wird verwendet,

- wenn man über **Vorhaben, Pläne, Absichten** für die Zukunft sprechen will.
- um auszudrücken, dass etwas **wahrscheinlich gleich geschehen wird** – es gibt bereits deutliche **Anzeichen** dafür (*hier:* die Wolken am Himmel).

5.2 The *will*-future

It will be cold and windy, and we will get some rain in the afternoon.
I'll be 15 next October.

I expect Ella will be late again as usual.
Ich nehme an, Ella kommt wie üblich wieder zu spät.

Just a moment. I'll open the door for you.
Moment. Ich mache Ihnen die Tür auf.
I won't tell anyone what's happened. I promise.
Ich sage niemandem, was passiert ist. ...

Das **Futur mit *will*** wird verwendet,

- um **Vorhersagen** über die Zukunft zu äußern. Oft geht es dabei um Dinge, die man nicht beeinflussen kann, z.B. das Wetter.
- um eine **Vermutung** auszudrücken (oft eingeleitet mit *I think, I'm sure, I expect, maybe*).
- wenn man sich **spontan** – also ohne es im Voraus geplant zu haben – zu etwas **entschließt**. Oft geht es dabei um **Hilfsangebote** oder **Versprechen**.

5.3 The present progressive (future meaning)

We're driving to Scotland next Friday to visit my grandparents.
I'm meeting a friend in town tonight.

Das ***present progressive*** wird verwendet, wenn etwas **für die Zukunft fest geplant** oder **fest verabredet** ist (manchmal spricht man vom *diary future*). Durch eine Zeitangabe wie *tonight* oder aus dem Zusammenhang muss klar sein, dass es um etwas Zukünftiges geht.

GF 7 The passive ► *p. 160*

7.3 Form

Das Passiv bildet man mit einer **Form von *be*** und der 3. Form des Verbs (Partizip Perfekt, *past participle*).

Simple present	I am often invited to parties.	... werde oft eingeladen
Simple past	The bridge was built in the 1950s.	... wurde gebaut
Present perfect	All the sandwiches have been eaten.	... sind gegessen worden
***will*-future**	Our new CD will be released next week.	... wird veröffentlicht werden
Modals	Mobile phones must be turned off now. Concert tickets can be bought online.	... müssen ausgeschaltet werden ... können gekauft werden

GF 9 Conditional sentences ► *p. 163*

9.1 Type 1

If you run, you'll catch the bus.
Wenn du rennst, kriegst du den Bus noch.

If you miss the bus, you can take / should take / must take a taxi.
Wenn du den Bus verpasst, kannst/sollst/musst du ein Taxi nehmen.

***if*-Satz (Bedingung)**	**Hauptsatz (Folge)**
If you run,	*you'll catch the bus.*
If you miss the bus,	*you can take a taxi.*
simple present	**– *will-future* – *can/should/must* + Infinitiv**

1 LISTENING Friends on the net

Richard B; Angie A; Robin E; Lisa C; Josie F

2 LISTENING Voicemail messages

1 T; *2* F; *3* N; *4* N; *5* F; *6* T; *7* T; *8* F; *9* F; *10* T; *11* N; *12* F

3 LISTENING Talking about free time

1 country *2* four thirty *3* twenty-five *4* grandmother *5* Seven, five thirty *6* mum/mother *7* Aussie rules *8* baseball *9* water *10* swimming/to the swimming club *11* Monday, five fifteen *12* 4.54

4 SPEAKING Dumped

1 surprised/shocked/upset by text message, doesn't understand what has happened, text message came suddenly, probably feeling hurt, unhappy, unwanted
2 has been dumped by a friend or boyfriend
3 **No** – text message not a good way to end a relationship, shows the person who sent it does not care much about feelings of other person, a person who gets dumped by text message maybe feels as if he/she was not very important to the partner
Yes – quick and easy way to end a relationship, no arguments, no hard words, no long explanation, no difficult situation, no crying, etc.; breaking up hurts anyway, so it doesn't matter how you do it
4 talk to a good friend, go out with others, join a club and meet new people, do hobbies

5 SPEAKING A cartoon

The cartoon shows a father talking to his teenage son, who is standing next to him. The father doesn't look very happy. Although he doesn't know what blogging is, he tells his son to stop it because he imagines it's something bad. The boy maybe thinks his father is strict without reason, and behind the times. The cartoon's message is that older people often don't know and don't trust modern electronic communication. This can make relationships between parents and teenagers difficult. I (don't) agree with the cartoon artist because ...

6 SPEAKING Comparing photos

Picture 1 shows three young people, two girls and a boy, who are sightseeing in London without family. They are looking at a guide book, maybe they are talking about where to go next.
Picture 2 shows a family of four (parents, son, daughter) on holiday in a sunny place. There is a swimming pool in the background. The four people are sitting at a table next to the pool. There are cakes, ice cream and soft drinks on the table. The atmosphere is relaxed.
Holidays with friends
Advantages: you can plan everything yourselves, you can do things that interest teenagers, it's fun being with good friends, you can stay up late, you can travel with just a rucksack, you can stay at youth hostels, it's good experience to be alone and do things for yourself
Disadvantages: there are no parents to help, pay, plan, drive or rent a car, you have to fit in with the rest of the group, it may not be easy being together with the same people every day, you may argue because each of you wants something different, you have to be organized, careful and look after all your things yourself
Holidays with parents
Advantages: they organize, plan, pay and drive, you can count on them if you need help or if there are problems, you can relax and not worry about planning, money, safety
Disadvantages: you may miss friends of your own age, you may have to do things that you are not very interested in, you may have to get up earlier than you hoped, you may argue

7 WRITING A questionnaire (Individual answers)

8 WRITING A picture story

Sophie's boyfriend dumped her by text message. She felt sad and angry. Did he have a new girlfriend now? She was crying when she phoned her best friend. The friend advised Sophie not to sit at home, but to go somewhere and do something. Sophie decided to visit her cousin at the weekend. She would go on her moped the next day. When she left home on her moped it was raining. An hour later she stopped at a café on the way. A nice young guy came in. He sat at the next table, and soon they were chatting and laughing. They left the café together. They would meet again the next day. Had Sophie forgotten her boyfriend already?

9, 10 WRITING What's your opinion? A report

(Individual answers)

11 MEDIATION A letter to a problem page

Was man tun soll:
eine neue Freundschaft suchen, alles loswerden, was an die Beziehung erinnert – E-mails, Fotos usw., sich mit irgendetwas beschäftigen, damit man abgelenkt ist; erst zu Bett gehen, wenn man sehr müde ist; Dinge unternehmen, wofür man früher keine Zeit hatte, mit Freunden/-innen über die Situation reden.
Was man nicht tun soll:
romantische Musik spielen, romantische Filme anschauen oder glücklichen Paaren zuschauen, Plätze aufsuchen, die Erinnerungen an die glückliche Zeit wachrufen

12 MEDIATION Adverts

four apprenticeships in Hamburg:
1 hairdresser in city centre, young team, can start immediately,
2 chef in a 4-star hotel kitchen, can start immediately, experience an advantage
3 car mechanic in large repair garage, have to have good GCSEs, should be interested in customer service, experience is an advantage
4 bank clerk, need good GCSEs in maths, German, English, must be reliable, should be interested in customer service, offer training, modern working place

13 READING Daniel's blog

b) *1* C; *2* C; *3* B; *4* B; *5* B
c) *1* T; *2* N; *3* N; *4* F; *5* T; *6* F; *7* T; *8* T; *9* N; *10* F
d) *1* Maria: Spanish; Sven: Swedish; Nina: British; Jean-Paul: French; Max: German; Elena: Greek; Anna: Polish
2 Daniel liked: his tennis and English course, the accommodation in college, the international atmosphere, the English breakfast, the conversation group, the Oxford city bus tour
3 Daniel didn't like: having to be in his room by 10.30 pm, the discussion on tennis tactics, strategy and mental attitude, the video analysis of how each student played

14 USE OF LANGUAGE A first date

a) *1* have changed *2* went *3* what *4* going *5* doing *6* at *7* to stand/standing *8* carefully *9* about 10 with 11 impression *12* yourself *13* make/tell *14* than *15* successful
b) *1* enjoy *2* wear *3* opinions *4* role *5* stupid *6* famous
c) *1* like *2* boring *3* interested *4* same *5* late *6* fantastic
d) *1* scary: A horror film for example is 'scary'.
2 advice: If you give somebody advice, you tell them what it is best to do or not to do in a situation.
3 opinion: Your opinion is what you think or feel about something or somebody.